For forty years Moses led his people through the dry, cruel desert. They did not hunger—for God gave them sweet manna from Heaven; they did not thirst—for God gave them sweet water to drink. Yet they still complained and even defied the commandments Moses had given them from God. But they were granted miracle after miracle and God kept His promise. They finally found the rich, free land they had dreamed of since their days of harsh bondage in Egypt.

Here is the second in the unique series that brings all of the excitement, drama and color of the Bible in words and pictures from the world's greatest, truest Book!

The Picture Bible for All Ages

VOLUME 2

THE PROMISED LAND

EXODUS 20: 1—1 SAMUEL 16: 19

Script by Iva Hoth

Illustrations by Andre Le Blanc

Bible Editor, C. Elvan Olmstead, Ph.D.

David C. Cook Publishing Co.
850 NORTH GROVE AVENUE • ELGIN, IL 60120
In Canada: David C. Cook Publishing (Canada) Ltd., Weston, Ontario M9L 1T4

THE PROMISED LAND
First printing, June 1973
Second printing, September 1973
Third printing, October 1973
Fourth printing, January 1974
© 1973 David C. Cook Publishing Co., Elgin, IL 60120
All Rights Reserved. This book, or parts thereof,
may not be reproduced in any form without permission
of the publisher, except by a reviewer who wishes
to quote brief passages in connection with a review
in a magazine or newspaper.
Published by David C. Cook Publishing Co.
Printed in United States of America by Offset Paperbacks.
Library of Congress Catalog Card Number: 73-78168
ISBN: 0-912692-14-6

ILLUSTRATED STORIES

THE PROMISED LAND

> *Arise, go over this Jordan,*
> *thou, and all this people,*
> *unto the land which I do give to them,*
> *even to the children of Israel.*
> *Every place that the sole of your foot*
> *shall tread upon,*
> *that have I given unto you.*
>
> JOSHUA 1: 2, 3

Commandments of God

FROM EXODUS 20—32: 19

WHILE THE PEOPLE OF ISRAEL STAND BEFORE MOUNT SINAI, GOD SPEAKS FROM THE MOUNTAIN AND GIVES THEM THE TEN COMMANDMENTS:

I AM THE LORD THY GOD...THOU SHALT HAVE NO OTHER GODS BEFORE ME.

THOU SHALT NOT MAKE UNTO THEE ANY GRAVEN IMAGE.

THOU SHALT NOT TAKE THE NAME OF THE LORD THY GOD IN VAIN.

REMEMBER THE SABBATH DAY, TO KEEP IT HOLY.

HONOUR THY FATHER AND THY MOTHER.

THOU SHALT NOT KILL.

THOU SHALT NOT COMMIT ADULTERY.

THOU SHALT NOT STEAL.

THOU SHALT NOT BEAR FALSE WITNESS...

THOU SHALT NOT COVET...ANYTHING THAT IS THY NEIGHBOUR'S.

GOD GIVES MOSES MORE LAWS, AND WHEN THESE ARE WRITTEN DOWN, MOSES BUILDS AN ALTAR. HE AND HIS PEOPLE MAKE AN AGREEMENT, OR COVENANT, WITH GOD. "ALL THAT THE LORD HATH SAID WILL WE DO", THE PEOPLE PROMISE.

LATER, GOD CALLS MOSES TO COME AGAIN TO MOUNT SINAI. JOSHUA GOES PART WAY WITH HIM. DAYS PASS, AND MOSES DOES NOT RETURN.

WHEN IS MOSES COMING BACK?

CAN WE GO LOOK FOR HIM?

WE DON'T KNOW—BUT YOU MUST NOT FOLLOW HIM UP THE MOUNTAIN. HE IS ALONE WITH GOD.

WHO KNOWS—MAYBE MOSES ISN'T COMING BACK...

IF HE DOESN'T, WHAT WILL WE DO?

LET'S ASK AARON TO MAKE US A STATUE THAT WE CAN WORSHIP.

YES—WE WANT A GOD WE CAN SEE.

FEELING LOST WITHOUT THEIR LEADER, THE PEOPLE FORGET GOD'S COMMANDMENTS AND THEIR PROMISE TO WORSHIP HIM ONLY. THEY BRING THEIR JEWELRY TO AARON WHO MELTS IT AND MAKES A GOLDEN STATUE OF A CALF.

11

OUR BIBLE IN PICTURES
Death to an Idol
FROM EXODUS 32: 20—40: 17

SHOCKED BY THE SIGHT OF MOSES BREAKING THE STONE TABLETS, THE PEOPLE STOP WORSHIPING THE GOLDEN CALF.

WHAT WILL MOSES DO TO US?

AARON, WHERE DID YOU GET THIS IDOL?

THE PEOPLE GAVE ME THEIR GOLD! I THREW IT INTO A FIRE, AND OUT CAME THIS GOLDEN CALF.

THROW IT BACK INTO THE FIRE!

WHEN THE GOLD-COVERED IDOL IS BURNED, MOSES GRINDS IT INTO POWDER AND THROWS IT INTO A STREAM.

NOW— DRINK THE WATER. ALL OF YOU!

DRINK IT?

IT TASTES AWFUL!

UGH!— IT WILL MAKE US SICK!

LET THIS BE A LESSON TO YOU. REMEMBER WHAT YOU HAVE DONE WHILE I GO BACK UP THE MOUNTAIN AND ASK GOD TO FORGIVE YOU!

HIGH ON THE MOUNTAIN, WHERE HE HAD RECEIVED GOD'S COMMANDMENTS, MOSES KNEELS TO PRAY.

LORD, IF YOU WILL, PLEASE FORGIVE THEM. BUT IF NOT, PUNISH ME, TOO.

GOD DOES FORGIVE HIS PEOPLE. MOSES SPENDS FORTY DAYS ON THE MOUNTAIN, WHILE GOD GIVES HIM MORE LAWS AND WRITES THE TEN COMMANDMENTS AGAIN ON TWO NEW TABLETS OF STONE.

14

BACK IN CAMP, THE PEOPLE PRAY FOR MOSES' SAFE RETURN. BUT WHEN THEY SEE HIM COMING DOWN THE MOUNTAIN, THEY ARE AFRAID...

IT'S MOSES! BUT LOOK AT HIS FACE—IT HAS A BRIGHTNESS LIKE THE SUNLIGHT!

THE GLORY OF HAVING BEEN WITH GOD SHINES ON MOSES' FACE. HE COVERS HIS FACE WITH A VEIL SO THAT THE PEOPLE WILL NOT BE FRIGHTENED.

COME—DO NOT BE AFRAID. GOD HAS FORGIVEN YOU.

AND HE HAS GIVEN ME PLANS FOR A TENT-HOUSE OF WORSHIP. BRING YOUR OFFERINGS AND WE WILL ALL WORK TOGETHER TO MAKE IT.

THE PEOPLE GLADLY BRING JEWELRY, CLOTH, SKINS, RARE METALS AND WOOD SO THAT GOD'S HOUSE WILL BE BEAUTIFUL.

16

The Tabernacle

FROM EXODUS 40: 18-38; LEVITICUS 1—10: 2

AFTER MANY WEEKS OF CAREFUL, LOVING WORK THE HOUSE OF GOD, THE TABERNACLE, IS READY...JOYOUSLY THE PEOPLE WATCH AS MOSES CARRIES THE SACRED ARK CONTAINING THE TEN COMMANDMENTS INTO THE TABERNACLE. HE PLACES IT IN A SPECIAL ROOM CALLED THE HOLY OF HOLIES. THEN A CLOUD COVERS THE TABERNACLE AND THE GLORY OF THE LORD FILLS IT.

NOW THE ISRAELITES ARE NO LONGER A MOB OF FLEEING SLAVES. IN THE ONE YEAR SINCE THEY LEFT EGYPT, THEY HAVE BECOME A NATION WITH LAWS, JUDGES AND A PLACE OF WORSHIP.

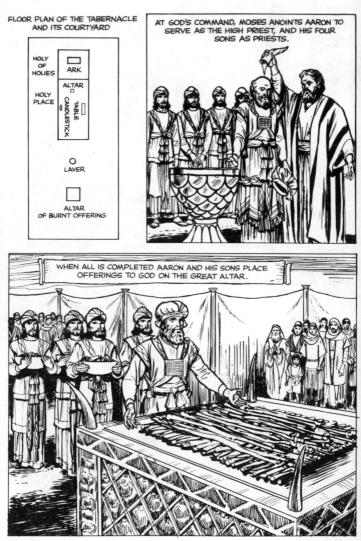

FLOOR PLAN OF THE TABERNACLE AND ITS COURTYARD

HOLY OF HOLIES — ARK

HOLY PLACE — ALTAR, TABLE, CANDLESTICK

LAVER

ALTAR OF BURNT OFFERING

AT GOD'S COMMAND, MOSES ANOINTS AARON TO SERVE AS THE HIGH PRIEST, AND HIS FOUR SONS AS PRIESTS.

WHEN ALL IS COMPLETED AARON AND HIS SONS PLACE OFFERINGS TO GOD ON THE GREAT ALTAR.

THE PEOPLE COME TO THE TABERNACLE TO WORSHIP, AND AS MOSES AND AARON BLESS THEM...

FIRE FROM HEAVEN! LOOK— IT'S BURNING THE OFFERING!

GOD COMMANDS THAT THE SACRED FIRE BE KEPT BURNING ON THE ALTAR, AND THAT THE ISRAELITES USE NO OTHER FIRE IN THEIR WORSHIP.

BUT ONE DAY TWO OF AARON'S SONS ARE DRUNK AS THEY GO TO THE TABERNACLE TO OFFER INCENSE. THEY CARRY WITH THEM COALS FROM THEIR FIRE AT HOME.

WHO WILL KNOW WHICH FIRE WE USE?

WHAT DIFFERENCE DOES IT MAKE? FIRE IS FIRE.

BUT AS THEY SPRINKLE INCENSE ON THE FIRE WHICH GOD HAD NOT TOLD THEM TO USE...

A FLAME LEAPS OUT...AND THE TWO PRIESTS DROP DEAD!

Pillar of Fire

FROM LEVITICUS 10: 3; NUMBERS 1-10

WHEN TWO OF AARON'S SONS GET DRUNK AND DISOBEY GOD'S COMMAND ABOUT WORSHIP IN THE TABERNACLE, THEY ARE STRUCK DEAD. THE WHOLE CAMP IS SHOCKED ...AND MOSES WARNS AARON AND THE OTHER TWO SONS.

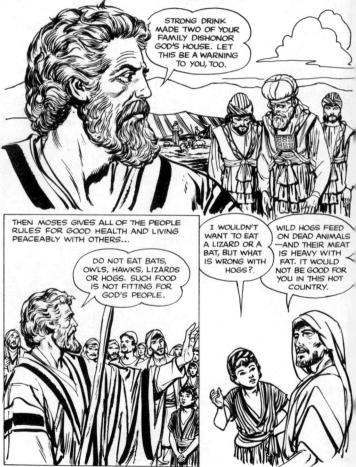

STRONG DRINK MADE TWO OF YOUR FAMILY DISHONOR GOD'S HOUSE. LET THIS BE A WARNING TO YOU, TOO.

THEN MOSES GIVES ALL OF THE PEOPLE RULES FOR GOOD HEALTH AND LIVING PEACEABLY WITH OTHERS...

DO NOT EAT BATS, OWLS, HAWKS, LIZARDS OR HOGS. SUCH FOOD IS NOT FITTING FOR GOD'S PEOPLE.

I WOULDN'T WANT TO EAT A LIZARD OR A BAT, BUT WHAT IS WRONG WITH HOGS?.

WILD HOGS FEED ON DEAD ANIMALS —AND THEIR MEAT IS HEAVY WITH FAT. IT WOULD NOT BE GOOD FOR YOU IN THIS HOT COUNTRY.

THE PEOPLE ARE DIVIDED INTO TWELVE TRIBES—BESIDES THE TRIBE OF LEVI WHICH IS SET APART FOR RELIGIOUS DUTIES. MOSES CALLS A MEETING OF THE TRIBAL LEADERS.

WHEN THE FIGHTING MEN HAVE BEEN COUNTED, A PLAN OF DEFENSE IS SET UP THAT WILL BE FOLLOWED IN CAMPING DURING THE LONG JOURNEY AHEAD. THE OUTER RIM OF THE CAMP IS MADE UP OF THE 12 TRIBES—3 ON EACH SIDE. IN THE CENTER IS THE TABERNACLE WITH PRIESTS AND MEN OF THE TRIBE OF LEVI STATIONED AROUND IT.

ABOVE THE TABERNACLE—AS A SYMBOL OF GOD'S PRESENCE—IS A CLOUD BY DAY AND A PILLAR OF FIRE BY NIGHT.

ALL OF THIS PREPARATION RAISES QUESTIONS IN THE CAMP.

DOES THIS MEAN WE'RE GETTING READY TO MOVE ON?

I HOPE SO. I CAN HARDLY WAIT TO GET TO THE PROMISED LAND.

BUT AS THE FIRST ANNIVERSARY OF THE DAY THE PEOPLE FLED FROM EGYPT APPROACHES, THEY STOP THEIR WORK AND MAKE READY TO CELEBRATE THIS GREAT DAY OF FREEDOM.

PUT ALL THE YEAST DOUGH IN THIS JAR—WE MUST PUT IT AWAY. FOR SEVEN DAYS WE ARE TO EAT BREAD WITHOUT YEAST—JUST AS WE DID WHEN THE ANGEL OF DEATH PASSED OVER OUR HOMES IN EGYPT.

23

Fire in Camp

FROM NUMBERS 10—11: 2

EXCITEMENT SPREADS THROUGH THE CAMP AS THE PEOPLE TALK MORE AND MORE ABOUT THE PROMISED LAND TO WHICH GOD IS LEADING THEM. ONE DAY THE BLAST OF TWO GREAT SILVER TRUMPETS FILLS THE AIR...

THAT IS A SIGNAL FOR ALL OF THE PEOPLE TO COME TO THE TABERNACLE. SOMETHING IMPORTANT MUST BE HAPPENING.

THE PEOPLE DROP WHAT THEY ARE DOING, AND HURRY TO THE TABERNACLE.

DOES THIS MEAN WE ARE GOING TO MOVE?

I DON'T KNOW. WE'LL HAVE TO WAIT AND SEE. OUR ORDERS COME FROM GOD.

WHEN EVERYONE HAS GATHERED...

LOOK! THE CLOUD IS LIFTING!

THE SIGN HAS BEEN GIVEN! EAGERLY THE PEOPLE LINE UP FOR THE MARCH TOWARD THE PROMISED LAND! LEADING THEM IS THE SACRED ARK, CARRIED BY THE PRIESTS.

24

HIGH ON A HILLTOP, MOSES WATCHES AS THE MARCH GETS UNDER WAY.

GOD IS LEADING US, SO WE HAVE NOTHING TO FEAR.

MOSES IS RIGHT—THEY HAVE NOTHING TO FEAR. AND EVEN THOUGH THEY MARCH THROUGH A WILDERNESS, GOD CONTINUES TO PROVIDE MANNA FOR THEM TO EAT.

...BUT AFTER SEVERAL DAYS, THE PEOPLE BEGIN TO COMPLAIN AGAIN...

HOW LONG HAVE WE BEEN EATING THIS STUFF?

I'M GETTING TIRED OF IT.

DON'T WE HAVE ANYTHING ELSE TO EAT?

NO! I KEEP THINKING ABOUT THE MELONS AND MEAT WE HAD IN EGYPT. HOW GOOD THEY WOULD TASTE!

SOMETIMES I WISH WE HAD NEVER LEFT EGYPT

ARE MY PEOPLE *NEVER* SATISFIED? WILL THEY *NEVER* TRUST GOD?

O GOD, WHY DO MY PEOPLE ALWAYS COMPLAIN? WHAT MUST I DO TO TEACH THEM TO TRUST IN YOU COMPLETELY?

SUDDENLY, LIGHTNING STRIKES THE EDGE OF THE CAMP.

THE PEOPLE ARE TERRIFIED. THEY RUSH TO MOSES...

HELP! THE CAMP IS ON FIRE!

A Family Divided

FROM NUMBERS 11: 2—12: 10

WHEN FIRE BREAKS OUT IN THE ISRAELITE CAMP, THE PEOPLE QUICKLY FORGET THEIR COMPLAINT ABOUT FOOD AND TRY TO BEAT BACK THE FLAMES.

DID GOD SEND THE LIGHTNING TO BURN OUR TENTS?

MAYBE IT'S A WARNING FOR US TO STOP OUR GRUMBLING ABOUT THE FOOD HE HAS GIVEN US.

HELP US, MOSES! THE WHOLE CAMP WILL BE LOST!

ONLY GOD CAN HELP YOU NOW. I'LL PRAY FOR YOU.

AND AS MOSES PRAYS, THE FIRE GOES OUT.

LOOK! THE FIRE IS OUT!

I SAW IT WITH MY OWN EYES! WHEN MOSES PRAYED, THE FIRE DIED OUT. FROM NOW ON, I WON'T COMPLAIN ABOUT ANYTHING MOSES ASKS US TO DO.

BUT MANY OF THE PEOPLE KEEP ON COMPLAINING BECAUSE GOD HAS NOT GIVEN THEM MEAT AS WELL AS MANNA TO EAT. MOSES PRAYS AGAIN TO ASK GOD FOR HELP.

THE LORD SAYS YOU WILL SOON HAVE MEAT—PLENTY OF IT.

HOW CAN ANYONE —EVEN GOD—FIND MEAT FOR ALL OF US IN THIS DESERT?

I DON'T KNOW— BUT MOSES SPEAKS THE TRUTH. I SAW THE FIRE DIE OUT WHEN HE ASKED GOD FOR HELP, SO I BELIEVE HIM WHEN HE SAYS GOD WILL SEND US MEAT!

SUDDENLY THE WIND BEGINS TO BLOW IN FROM THE SEA...AND WITH IT COME GREAT FLOCKS OF QUAIL THAT COVER THE SKY LIKE A CLOUD.

AS THE QUAIL LAND ON THE DESERT, THE ISRAELITES PICK UP ALL THEY CAN CARRY.

MEAT! ALL WE CAN EAT!

LET'S STORE UP ALL WE CAN TO EAT LATER ON.

HOW MANY MORE BASKETS DO I HAVE TO GATHER?

GET AS MANY AS YOU CAN. AT LEAST _WE'LL_ HAVE ALL _WE_ NEED.

THE PEOPLE STUFF THEMSELVES UNTIL MANY ARE SICK.

IT SERVES ME RIGHT. I WAS TOO GREEDY.

SOON AFTER THIS, THE ORDER IS GIVEN TO CONTINUE THE JOURNEY. ONCE AGAIN, A CLOUD BY DAY AND A PILLAR OF FIRE BY NIGHT LEAD THE PEOPLE...TO A CAMP SITE CLOSER TO THEIR PROMISED HOMELAND.

NO SOONER IS CAMP SET UP THAN MOSES' OWN BROTHER AND SISTER TURN AGAINST HIM.

MOSES ACTS AS IF HE IS THE ONLY SPOKESMAN FOR GOD. HE SEEMS TO FORGET, AARON, THAT YOU ARE THE HIGH PRIEST.

29

YOU'RE RIGHT, MIRIAM. IT'S TIME WE HAVE A TALK WITH OUR BROTHER.

IN ANGER, THEY GO TO MOSES...

WE'RE TIRED OF HAVING YOU RUN EVERYTHING, MOSES. DO YOU THINK YOU ARE THE ONLY ONE WHO CAN SPEAK FOR GOD? DIDN'T GOD CALL AARON TO BE THE HIGH PRIEST? AND DON'T FORGET, I AM A PROPHETESS, TOO!

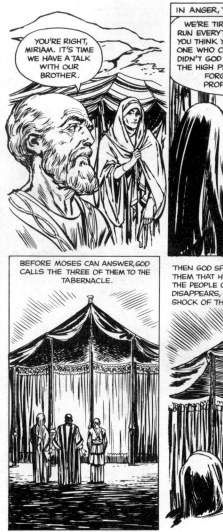

BEFORE MOSES CAN ANSWER, GOD CALLS THE THREE OF THEM TO THE TABERNACLE.

THEN GOD SPEAKS FROM A CLOUD, AND TELLS THEM THAT HE HAS CHOSEN MOSES TO LEAD THE PEOPLE OF ISRAEL. WHEN THE CLOUD DISAPPEARS, MIRIAM AND AARON GET THE SHOCK OF THEIR LIVES.

OUR BIBLE IN PICTURES

Revolt

FROM NUMBERS 12: 11—14: 10

IN A FIT OF JEALOUSY, MIRIAM AND AARON ACCUSE THEIR BROTHER, MOSES, OF ACTING AS IF HE WERE GOD'S ONLY SPOKESMAN. GOD ANSWERS THEIR ANGRY WORDS AND TELLS MIRIAM AND AARON THAT MOSES IS HIS CHOSEN LEADER. WHEN GOD FINISHES SPEAKING, MIRIAM DISCOVERS THAT SHE HAS LEPROSY- THE DISEASE MOST DREADED BY THE ISRAELITES.

OH! NO! WHY DID I SPEAK AGAINST MOSES? HELP ME! HELP ME!

WE WERE WRONG, MOSES. BUT DO NOT HOLD IT AGAINST US— PLEASE! CAN'T YOU HELP MIRIAM?

ONLY GOD CAN HEAL HER, AARON. BUT I WILL PRAY FOR OUR SISTER.

HEAL HER NOW, O GOD, I BEG OF THEE.

MIRIAM IS HEALED, BUT SHE IS BANISHED FROM THE CAMP FOR SEVEN DAYS.

ON THE SEVENTH DAY MIRIAM RETURNS, AND AARON, AS HIGH PRIEST, ACCEPTS HER BACK INTO THE CAMP.

I HAVE LEARNED MY LESSON, AARON.

SO HAVE I. LET US NEVER AGAIN DOUBT OR QUESTION GOD'S WISDOM.

THE ISRAELITES CONTINUE THEIR JOURNEY UNTIL THEY REACH THE WILDERNESS OF PARAN. THERE MOSES ORDERS THEM TO SET UP CAMP.

MEDITERRANEAN SEA

EGYPT

RED SEA

CANAAN

CAMP WILDERNESS OF PARAN

MT. SINAI

MIDIAN

Jordan R.

SEA OF GALILEE

DEAD SEA

ARABIAN DESERT

MOSES CALLS A MAN FROM EACH OF THE TRIBES TO ATTEND AN IMPORTANT MEETING.

WE ARE ON THE BORDER OF CANAAN, THE LAND GOD HAS PROMISED TO US. BUT BEFORE WE GO INTO IT, WE MUST KNOW WHAT LIES AHEAD.

WHAT ARE YOUR PLANS?

WE NEED TO EXPLORE THE LAND, JOSHUA. WE MUST FIND OUT WHAT THE PEOPLE ARE LIKE, HOW MANY RIVERS WE WILL HAVE TO CROSS, HOW WELL THE CITIES ARE FORTIFIED. IT'S A DANGEROUS JOB...BUT IT MUST BE DONE.

EACH MAN HERE CAN ACT AS A SCOUT, AND WE'LL GET STARTED RIGHT AWAY.

AT DAYBREAK THE SCOUTS SET OUT—SPREADING OUT TO COVER THE MAIN AREAS OF THE LAND BEFORE THEM.

LOOK AT THAT CITY!

AND THE SIZE OF THOSE WALLS!

33

34

Rebellion

FROM NUMBERS 14: 10—16: 5

JOSHUA PLEADS WITH THE PEOPLE TO HAVE COURAGE AND TAKE CANAAN, THE LAND GOD HAS PROMISED THEM. BUT THE PEOPLE ARE FRIGHTENED BY THE TEN COWARDLY SCOUTS WHO REPORT GIANTS AND FORTIFIED CITIES. ANGRILY THE PEOPLE TURN AGAINST JOSHUA AND HIS FELLOW SCOUT, CALEB.

STONE THEM!

DOWN WITH JOSHUA!

BUT SUDDENLY...

LOOK OVER THERE — THE TABERNACLE IS BURNING!

DON'T BE AFRAID — THE TABERNACLE IS **NOT** ON FIRE. IT GLOWS LIKE THAT BECAUSE GOD IS THERE TALKING TO MOSES.

36

38

erpents in the Wilderness

FROM NUMBERS 16: 5—21: 6

KORAH AND SOME OF HIS FRIENDS LED REVOLT AGAINST MOSES AND MOSES PROMISED THEM THAT ON THE FOLLOWING DAY GOD WOULD POINT OUT HIS CHOSEN LEADER. THE MOMENT HAS COME...

DEPART FROM KORAH AND THE MEN WHO WOULD LEAD YOU TO EVIL, LEST YOU LOSE YOUR LIVES. IF GOD HAS CHOSEN ME TO LEAD YOU, THE EARTH WILL OPEN AND SWALLOW THEM UP:.

AS MOSES SPEAKS, THERE IS A GREAT EARTHQUAKE, AND THE TENTS OF KORAH AND HIS FOLLOWERS FALL INTO A DEEP CRACK IN THE EARTH

THE FRIGHTENED PEOPLE TURN ONCE AGAIN TO MOSES. AS GOD COMMANDED, MOSES LEADS THEM AWAY FROM THE PROMISED LAND... TO WANDER FOR YEARS IN THE WILDERNESS.

WHEN HARDSHIPS COME, THEY FORGET THAT IT WAS THEIR FEAR THAT KEPT THEM FROM TAKING THE GOOD LAND GOD HAD PROMISED THEM. AGAIN AND AGAIN THEY COMPLAIN...

NO WATER! NOW WHAT WILL I DO?

THE SPRING IS DRY! HOW CAN I COOK—OR WASH?

OUR TRIBAL LEADERS WILL TAKE THIS UP WITH MOSES!

WELL, MOSES, WHERE ARE WE GOING TO GET WATER?

DID YOU LEAD US OUT HERE TO DIE OF THIRST?

LET'S GO BACK TO EGYPT—AT LEAST WE HAD FOOD AND WATER THERE.

ONCE AGAIN, MOSES AND HIS BROTHER, AARON, TAKE THEIR PROBLEM TO GOD. AND GOD TELLS THEM EXACTLY WHAT TO DO.

40

BUT MOSES IS STILL SO ANGRY WITH HIS PEOPLE THAT HE DISREGARDS GOD'S COMMAND AND STRIKES THE ROCK—TWICE— INSTEAD OF SPEAKING TO IT. WATER GUSHES OUT, AND THE PEOPLE DRINK HAPPILY.

BUT GOD IS DISPLEASED. HOW CAN MOSES AND AARON TEACH THE PEOPLE TO OBEY GOD IF THEY THEMSELVES DO NOT FOLLOW GOD'S INSTRUCTIONS? BECAUSE OF THE BAD EXAMPLE THEY HAVE SET, GOD TELLS THEM THAT NEITHER ONE SHALL ENTER THE PROMISED LAND.

THE ISRAELITES TRAVEL ON. WHEN THEY COME TO MOUNT HOR, GOD TELLS MOSES THAT AARON WILL SOON DIE, AND THAT HE SHOULD TAKE AARON AND HIS SON, ELEAZAR, TO THE MOUNTAINTOP.

ELEAZAR WILL TAKE YOUR PLACE AS HIGH PRIEST, AARON. I WILL PUT YOUR ROBES ON HIM.

AARON DIES ON MOUNT HOR, AND THE ISRAELITES MOURN FOR THIRTY DAYS. THEN THEY MOVE ON. A CLOUD LEADS THEM BY DAY, AND A PILLAR OF FIRE BY NIGHT.

BUT THE PEOPLE SOON FORGET GOD'S CARE... AND AGAIN THEY COMPLAIN...

THERE'S NOT ENOUGH WATER— I'M ALWAYS THIRSTY.

HAS NOT GOD ALWAYS GIVEN US WATER WHEN WE NEEDED IT?

YES, BUT—THE FOOD— I'M SICK OF THIS STUFF THAT MUST BE GATHERED EVERY DAY AND MADE INTO BREAD. I WANT FOOD LIKE WE HAD IN EGYPT— MELONS, FRUIT...

IN EGYPT YOU WERE BEATEN AND MADE TO WORK LIKE SLAVES. AND YOU CRIED FOR FREEDOM.

AND _YOU_ SAID GOD WOULD GIVE US FREEDOM! DO YOU CALL _THIS_ FREEDOM—WANDERING AROUND IN THE WILDERNESS?

SUDDENLY—AS PUNISHMENT FOR THEIR GRUMBLING—THE CAMP BECOMES ALIVE WITH POISONOUS SNAKES.

HELP! I'VE BEEN BITTEN!

MEANTIME—IN KING SIHON'S PALACE.

ATTACK THE ISRAELITES AT ONCE. WE'LL CATCH THEM OFF GUARD AND DESTROY THEM ALL.

IN A FEW HOURS, THE GREAT ARMY OF SIHON IS ON THE MARCH.

IN THE ISRAELITE CAMP, MOSES AND JOSHUA LISTEN TO THE REPORTS OF THE MESSENGERS...

THEY MIGHT TRY TO ATTACK US...LET'S GET READY, JUST IN CASE THEY COME...

DURING THE NIGHT KING SIHON AND HIS MEN SPY OUT THE ISRAELITE CAMP.

WE'LL ATTACK JUST BEFORE SUNRISE!

AT DAYBREAK—KING SIHON STRIKES AND IS MET WITH A SURPRISE COUNTERATTACK FROM THE ISRAELITES.

THE AMORITES ARE DEFEATED IN A SWIFT BATTLE. THEN JOSHUA GOES ON TO TAKE THE ENEMY'S CAPITAL CITY OF HESHBON.

THE ISRAELITE SOLDIERS ARE EAGER TO PUSH ON, AFTER THIS VICTORY, BUT JOSHUA GOES TO MOSES FOR ADVICE.

SHALL WE MOVE NORTH INTO BASHAN? IT IS A POWERFUL COUNTRY WITH A GIANT FOR A KING.

SEND OUT SOME SCOUTS TO EXPLORE THE LAND FIRST, JOSHUA. THEN WE WILL DECIDE.

JOSHUA'S SCOUTS ARE DISCOVERED, AND A MESSENGER HURRIES TO TELL KING OG OF BASHAN.

O KING, I SAW SOME STRANGE MEN SPYING OUT OUR LAND.

THEY MUST BE THE ISRAELITES. THEY'VE JUST CONQUERED THE AMORITES, BUT **WE'LL** TEACH THEM A LESSON...

A New Leader

FROM NUMBERS 21: 33—27: 18

BOLDLY THE GIANT KING OG OF BASHAN SETS OUT TO TEACH THE ISRAELITES A LESSON IN WARFARE. BUT HE SOON FINDS HE IS NO MATCH FOR JOSHUA. OG'S ARMY IS BEATEN. HE TRIES TO ESCAPE...

AFTER HIM, MEN! CATCH HIM!

MEDITERRANEAN SEA

SEA OF GALILEE

BASHAN

CANAAN

RIVER JABBOK

JORDAN RIVER

AMMONITES

JERICHO •

PLAINS OF MOAB

AMORITES

DEAD SEA

RIVER ARNON

MOAB

BROOK ZERED

THE KING IS CAPTURED, AND THE ISRAELITES TAKE THE COUNTRY.

AFTER CONQUERING THE AMORITES AND BASHAN, THE ISRAELITES SET UP THEIR TENTS ON THE PLAINS OF MOAB.

48

49

OUR THREE TRIBES ARE READY TO SETTLE DOWN HERE AND BUILD OUR HOMES. DO WE HAVE YOUR PERMISSION?

YOU HELPED TO CONQUER THIS LAND, AND YOU MAY HAVE IT. BUT FIRST WE'LL NEED YOU TO HELP US CONQUER THE LAND THAT LIES AHEAD.

WE'LL HELP, MOSES.

YES, YOU CAN COUNT ON US.

FOR THE SECOND TIME THE ISRAELITES HAVE COME TO THE BORDER OF THE PROMISED LAND. THIS TIME THEY ARE NOT AFRAID. MEN TALK OF THE FLOCKS AND HERDS THEY WILL HAVE...AND WOMEN DREAM OF PEACEFUL HOMES IN THE LAND WHICH GOD HAS PROMISED THEM.

ONE DAY MOSES CALLS JOSHUA TO AN IMPORTANT MEETING...

GOD HAS TOLD ME THAT MY WORK HERE ON EARTH IS ALMOST FINISHED, JOSHUA. A NEW LEADER WILL TAKE OUR PEOPLE INTO THE PROMISED LAND.

A NEW LEADER? OH, NO, MOSES! WHO COULD EVER TAKE YOUR PLACE?

YOU— JOSHUA!

THEN, BEFORE ALL THE MULTITUDE OF ISRAEL, JOSHUA KNEELS BEFORE MOSES.

THE LORD WILL BE WITH YOU, JOSHUA. BE STRONG AND BRAVE AND LEAD OUR PEOPLE TO THE PROMISED LAND.

A FEW DAYS LATER MOSES GIVES A LARGE SCROLL TO THE PRIESTS.

THIS IS A COPY OF GOD'S LAWS. PUT IT WITH THE HOLY ARK THAT HOLDS THE TABLETS OF STONE ON WHICH THE TEN COMMANDMENTS ARE WRITTEN.

MOSES AGAIN CALLS THE PEOPLE TOGETHER. THEY COME SADLY BECAUSE EVERYONE KNOWS THIS WILL BE HIS FAREWELL... HE CHANTS A SONG HE HAS WRITTEN...THEN HE RAISES HIS HAND IN BENEDICTION...

THE BLESSING OF GOD BE WITH YOU ALWAYS.

SLOWLY...MOSES TURNS AND WALKS AWAY...

THE AGED LEADER CLIMBS MOUNT NEBO AND GAZES DOWN ON THE LAND GOD HAS PROMISED HIS PEOPLE —AND THERE—ALONE WITH GOD—HE DIES.

BACK IN CAMP JOSHUA PRAYS TO GOD FOR HELP, AND THE LORD ANSWERS: BE NOT AFRAID, FOR THE LORD THY GOD IS WITH THEE.

THE ISRAELITES MOURN THIRTY DAYS FOR MOSES. THEN, JOSHUA CALLS A MEETING.

THE CAMPAIGNS AHEAD WILL BE HARD AND DANGEROUS. BUT I'LL SEEK GOD'S GUIDANCE IN EVERYTHING WE DO.

AND WE WILL FOLLOW YOU AS WE DID MOSES!

THREE DAYS FROM NOW WE WILL CROSS THE JORDAN RIVER. THEN WE MUST CAPTURE THE CITY OF JERICHO—BUT FIRST WE NEED TO LEARN ALL WE CAN ABOUT IT.

54

THE SPIES PROMISE SAFETY TO RAHAB AND HER FAMILY.

56

HIDE OUT IN THE MOUNTAINS FOR THREE DAYS—AFTER THAT IT WILL BE SAFE FOR YOU TO CROSS THE RIVER TO YOUR OWN CAMP.

WHEN THE ATTACK COMES, KEEP YOUR FAMILY IN THE HOUSE ...AND TIE THIS RED ROPE IN YOUR WINDOW SO OUR MEN WILL KNOW WHERE YOU LIVE!

THE SPIES OBEY RAHAB—AND AFTER THREE DAYS, MAKE THEIR REPORT TO JOSHUA.

THE CITY IS WELL DEFENDED WITH TWO WALLS—EACH THIRTY FEET HIGH. THE OUTER WALL IS SIX FEET THICK AND THE INNER TWELVE.

BUT THE PEOPLE HAVE HEARD OF US AND THEY ARE AFRAID.

GOOD WORK, MEN. WE'LL GO AHEAD WITH OUR PLANS TO CROSS THE JORDAN AND TAKE JERICHO.

THE RIVER IS SWIFT AND WIDE—HOW CAN WE CROSS IT?

GOD HELPED OUR PEOPLE CROSS THE RED SEA. LET'S TRUST HIM TO HELP US NOW.

Siege of Jericho

FROM JOSHUA 4: 1—6: 20

AS IF HELD BACK BY A GIANT HAND, THE WATERS OF THE JORDAN STOP FLOWING WHILE THE ISRAELITES CROSS OVER INTO THE PROMISED LAND. WHEN ALL HAVE CROSSED, JOSHUA ORDERS A MAN FROM EACH OF THE TRIBES TO BRING A LARGE STONE FROM THE RIVER BED.

CARRY THESE STONES TO CAMP. THEY WILL REMIND US OF HOW GOD STOPPED THE JORDAN SO THAT WE MIGHT CROSS OVER SAFELY.

THEN JOSHUA SETS UP 12 OTHER STONES IN THE MIDDLE OF THE JORDAN — AT THE PLACE WHERE THE PRIESTS HOLD THE ARK. AFTER THAT HE COMMANDS THE PRIESTS TO CARRY THE ARK ACROSS. WHEN THEY REACH THE BANK THE FLOOD WATERS OF THE JORDAN RUSH FORTH...

THE ISRAELITES SET UP THEIR FIRST CAMP AT GILGAL—AND HERE THEY CELEBRATE THEIR FIRST PASSOVER FEAST IN THE PROMISED LAND.

AND HERE, TOO, THEY FIND FRUIT AND GRAIN.

LOOK! FOOD—ENOUGH FOR EVERYONE!

THANK GOD—THIS IS TRULY A WONDERFUL LAND.

NOW THAT THE PEOPLE CAN FIND FOOD FOR THEMSELVES, GOD NO LONGER SENDS THE MANNA WHICH HE HAS FURNISHED THEM SINCE THEY LEFT EGYPT FORTY YEARS AGO.

WHILE THE REST OF THE CAMP IS ENJOYING THE NEW LAND, JOSHUA SCOUTS THE AREA IN PREPARATION FOR THE ATTACK ON JERICHO. SUDDENLY HE LOOKS UP AND SEES A MAN WITH A SWORD!

IS HE GOING TO TRY TO KILL ME?

BUT JOSHUA IS NO COWARD—BRAVELY HE FACES THE STRANGER.

ARE YOU FRIEND—OR ENEMY?

I AM THE CAPTAIN OF THE LORD'S ARMY!

WHAT IS IT YOU WANT TO TELL ME?

REMOVE YOUR SHOES—FOR THE PLACE WHERE YOU STAND IS HOLY GROUND.

JOSHUA OBEYS—

HERE IS WHAT YOU MUST DO TO TAKE THE CITY OF JERICHO—

WHEN THE ANGEL LEAVES, JOSHUA RETURNS TO CAMP AND CALLS THE PRIESTS TOGETHER.

I WANT THE ARK CARRIED AROUND THE WALLS OF JERICHO. SEVEN PRIESTS WITH TRUMPETS WILL MARCH AHEAD OF IT.

ONCE A DAY FOR SIX DAYS STRAIGHT JOSHUA MARCHES THE ISRAELITES AROUND THE CITY OF JERICHO. FROM HER HOUSE ON THE WALL RAHAB WATCHES ANXIOUSLY...

THE ISRAELITES GIVE NO SIGN OF ATTACK—YET THE CITY IS BREATHLESS WITH FEAR.

61

AND IN THE GUARD TOWER, JERICHO SOLDIERS GROW TENSE...

WHAT ARE THEY TRYING TO DO—WORK AN EVIL CHARM ON US?

WHATEVER IT IS —IT'S WORKING. OUR SOLDIERS ARE SCARED!

ON THE SEVENTH DAY THE ISRAELITES MARCH AROUND JERICHO SEVEN TIMES. THE PRIESTS BLOW THEIR TRUMPETS—THE MARCHERS SHOUT—AND...

Attack that Failed

FROM JOSHUA 6: 20—7: 4

64

BUT ONE SOLDIER, ACHAN, COVETS THE THINGS HE SEES.

WHY SHOULD I FIGHT FOR A CITY AND NOT TAKE SOME OF THE SPOIL? I'LL HIDE THESE, AND NO ONE WILL KNOW...

THAT NIGHT WHILE THE REST OF THE CAMP SLEEPS HE BURIES HIS STOLEN TREASURE.

THIS WILL HELP ME GET STARTED IN THIS NEW LAND.

FINALLY JERICHO IS SET ON FIRE... AND FROM A DISTANT HILLTOP JOSHUA AND HIS MEN WATCH.

SOON THERE WILL BE NOTHING LEFT OF A ONCE POWERFUL CITY.

IT WAS SO WICKED THAT IT HAD TO BE DESTROYED OR ITS EVIL WAYS WOULD HAVE SPREAD AMONG OUR PEOPLE.

THE NEXT DAY, JOSHUA CALLS SOME OF HIS SCOUTS TO HIM.

HERE LIES THE CITY OF AI—IT GUARDS THE APPROACH TO OUR FUTURE CAMPAIGNS. WE MUST FIND OUT HOW STRONG THE CITY IS BEFORE WE ATTACK IT.

WE'LL SCOUT IT OUT AS WE DID JERICHO.

65

66

Tricked

FROM JOSHUA 7: 5—9: 16

THE FRIGHTENED ISRAELITES RETURN FROM THEIR DEFEAT AT AI. JOSHUA AND THE WHOLE CAMP ARE STUNNED!

WHAT HAPPENED?

I DON'T KNOW—ALL OF A SUDDEN I WAS AFRAID—AND RAN.

IT WAS AWFUL! THE SOLDIERS OF AI CHASED US ALL THE WAY TO THE STONE QUARRIES.

BUT WHY? WHY WERE YOU AFRAID? WHY DID YOU RUN?

THE SOLDIERS CANNOT ANSWER, SO JOSHUA SEEKS HELP FROM GOD.

O GOD, WHY DID THIS HAPPEN TO US? NOW OUR ENEMIES WILL DESTROY US.

GOD REPLIES THAT THE PEOPLE ARE BEING PUNISHED BECAUSE SOMEONE DISOBEYED HIM WHEN THEY TOOK JERICHO.

EARLY THE NEXT MORNING JOSHUA CALLS THE LEADERS OF THE TRIBES TO HIM.

SOMEONE DISOBEYED GOD'S ORDER AND KEPT PART OF THE SPOILS OF JERICHO FOR HIMSELF. THAT MAN MUST BE PUNISHED— OR WE WILL DIE AT THE HANDS OF THE ENEMY.

GOD POINTS OUT ACHAN AS THE GUILTY ONE.

IT IS TRUE—I SINNED AGAINST GOD AND MY PEOPLE.

NOW WE STAND RIGHT WITH GOD.

THAT SAME DAY JOSHUA CALLS HIS LEADERS TO HIM AGAIN.

TAKE THIRTY THOUSAND MEN AND HIDE THEM WEST OF AI. DO NOT ATTACK UNTIL I GIVE THE SIGNAL.

UNDER COVER OF DARKNESS THE ISRAELITES HIDE OUT AROUND AI.

WHAT IS JOSHUA'S PLAN?

I DON'T KNOW —BUT THIS TIME I'M NOT AFRAID. WITH GOD'S HELP WE WILL NOT FAIL.

69

70

JOSHUA MARCHES HIS SOLDIERS ALL NIGHT— AND CATCHES THE ENEMY FORCES AROUND GIBEON BY SURPRISE.

DON'T LET A MAN ESCAPE!

FLEEING FROM THE ISRAELITES, THE ENEMY IS CAUGHT IN A TERRIBLE HAILSTORM.

JOSHUA IS AFRAID THE ENEMY WILL ESCAPE DURING THE NIGHT SO HE COMMANDS THE SUN AND MOON TO STAND STILL...

AND DAYLIGHT LASTS UNTIL JOSHUA WINS THE VICTORY. THE PEOPLE OF GIBEON ARE SAVED, BUT THE PRICE OF THEIR TRICK ALLIANCE IS THAT THEY MUST WORK AS SERVANTS FOR THE ISRAELITES.

UNDER JOSHUA THE ISRAELITES CONQUER ALL OF THE CITIES OF SOUTHERN CANAAN. THEN THEY GO BACK TO THEIR CAMP AT GILGAL.

PRAISE THE LORD. PEACE AT LAST!

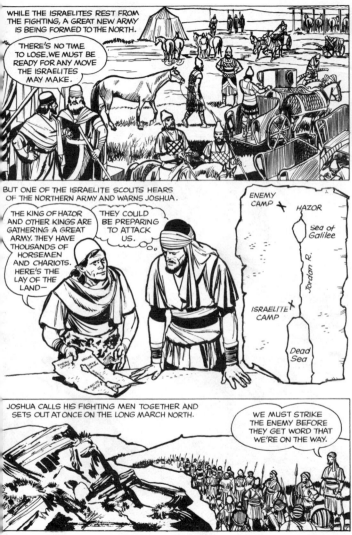

WHILE THE ISRAELITES REST FROM THE FIGHTING, A GREAT NEW ARMY IS BEING FORMED TO THE NORTH.

THERE'S NO TIME TO LOSE. WE MUST BE READY FOR ANY MOVE THE ISRAELITES MAY MAKE.

BUT ONE OF THE ISRAELITE SCOUTS HEARS OF THE NORTHERN ARMY AND WARNS JOSHUA.

THE KING OF HAZOR AND OTHER KINGS ARE GATHERING A GREAT ARMY. THEY HAVE THOUSANDS OF HORSEMEN AND CHARIOTS. HERE'S THE LAY OF THE LAND—

THEY COULD BE PREPARING TO ATTACK US.

ENEMY CAMP
HAZOR
Sea of Galilee
Jordan R.
ISRAELITE CAMP
Dead Sea

JOSHUA CALLS HIS FIGHTING MEN TOGETHER AND SETS OUT AT ONCE ON THE LONG MARCH NORTH.

WE MUST STRIKE THE ENEMY BEFORE THEY GET WORD THAT WE'RE ON THE WAY.

Traitors to God

FROM JOSHUA 11: 8—JUDGES 4: 2

WHEN JOSHUA LEARNS THAT THE NORTHERN KINGS ARE FORMING A GREAT ARMY, HE MAKES A QUICK MARCH NORTH AND CATCHES THEM OFF GUARD. HIS LIGHTNING ATTACK THROWS THE ENEMY INTO PANIC.

WHAT HAPPENED?

WE'VE BEEN ATTACKED!

WE'RE SURROUNDED!

WITH QUICK, DECISIVE BLOWS, JOSHUA TAKES THE CAMP. SOME OF THE ENEMY TRY TO ESCAPE, BUT ISRAELITE SOLDIERS FOLLOW IN CLOSE PURSUIT. THE FIGHTING LASTS THROUGHOUT THE DAY, BUT BY NIGHTFALL THE ENEMY IS IN JOSHUA'S HANDS.

WHEN THE WAR IS OVER, THE ISRAELITES REJOICE AND GIVE THANKS TO GOD FOR THEIR VICTORIES. THEN JOSHUA CALLS THE LEADERS TO A SPECIAL MEETING.

WE HAVE WON MUCH OF THE LAND GOD PROMISED US; IT IS TIME FOR US TO DIVIDE IT AMONG THE TRIBES.

CALEB, JOSHUA'S FRIEND, SPEAKS FIRST.

BECAUSE I WAS ONE OF THE SCOUTS WHO WAS NOT AFRAID TO TAKE CANAAN 45 YEARS AGO, GOD PROMISED THAT SOMEDAY I COULD HAVE THE LAND I SAW.

GIVE ME THE LAND AROUND MT. HEBRON AND I WILL DRIVE OFF THE GIANTS WHO LIVE THERE AND MAKE IT MY HOME.

YOUR WISH IS GRANTED, CALEB. AND MAY GOD BLESS YOU.

THE LAND OF CANAAN IS DIVIDED AMONG THE TRIBES OF ISRAEL.

MEDITERRANEAN SEA

ASHER

NAPHTALI

ZEBULUN

ISSACHAR

SEA OF GALILEE

JORDAN R.

MANASSEH

MANASSEH

EPHRAIM

DAN

GAD

BENJAMIN

JUDAH

REUBEN

DEAD SEA

SIMEON

SOME YEARS AFTER THE PEOPLE ARE SETTLED IN THEIR NEW HOMELAND, JOSH AGAIN CALLS THE TRIBAL LEADERS TO H

I AM OLD AND HAVE LITTLE TIME LEFT TO SERVE AS YOUR LEADER. LET ME REMIND YOU OF ALL THAT GOD HAS DONE FOR YOU. CHOOSE THIS DAY WHOM YOU WILL SERVE. WILL IT BE GOD, OR FALSE IDOLS?

THE LORD OUR GOD WILL WE SERVE, AND HIS VOICE WILL WE OBEY!

JOSHUA DIES, AND FOR A LONG TIME HIS LEADERS KEEP THEIR PLEDGE TO GOD. THEY BUILD UP STRONG CITIES AND JUDGES ARE CHOSEN TO RULE OVER THEM. BUT WHEN JOSHUA'S FRIENDS GROW OLD AND DIE, MANY OF THE ISRAELITES FORGET GOD...

AND BEGIN TO WORSHIP THE IDOLS OF THEIR NEIGHBORS...

AS A RESULT, THE ISRAELITES BECOME SO WEAK THAT THEY CANNOT DEFEND THEMSELVES AGAINST THE ATTACKS OF THEIR NEIGHBORS. TIME AND AGAIN ISRAELITE JUDGES LEAD THEIR PEOPLE BACK TO GOD AND VICTORY. BUT THE PEOPLE'S FAITH IS WEAK; WHEN THEY TURN AGAIN TO WORSHIP HEATHEN IDOLS THEY ARE INVADED BY KING JABIN'S RAIDERS...

Battle in the Storm

FROM JUDGES 4—5

AGAIN THE ISRAELITES FORGET ALL THAT GOD HAS DONE FOR THEM AND TURN TO WORSHIP THE IDOLS OF THEIR NEIGHBORS. SOON THEY BECOME SO WEAK AND AFRAID THEY CAN'T EVEN PROTECT THEIR OWN FIELDS FROM CANAANITE RAIDERS.

STOP! THAT'S MY GRAIN!

IT'S OURS NOW—SO, WHAT ARE YOU GOING TO DO ABOUT IT?

YEARS AGO OUR GREAT LEADER, JOSHUA, CONQUERED THE CANAANITES. NOW THEY ARE CONQUERING US!

WHAT'S THE MATTER WITH OUR LEADERS? WE'LL STARVE IF KING JABIN'S MEN KEEP STEALING OUR GRAIN.

ONE FIELD AFTER ANOTHER IS RAIDED UNTIL AT LAST THE FARMERS HAVE A MEETING.

SOMETHING MUST BE DONE AT ONCE— TO STOP THOSE CANAANITES.

LET'S GO IN A BODY TO SEE DEBORAH.

THE ANGRY FARMERS TAKE THEIR STORY TO DEBORAH, WHO IS THE JUDGE OF ISRAEL.

WHAT CAN WE DO—THE CANAANITES ARE STEALING ALL OUR FOOD.

GOD WILL HELP US—IF WE TRUST HIM.

DEBORAH ACTS SWIFTLY...

TAKE A MESSAGE TO CAPTAIN BARAK IN THE NORTH COUNTRY. TELL HIM TO COME AT ONCE.

THIS SOUNDS LIKE WAR.

WE DON'T HAVE A CHANCE AGAINST THE CANAANITES. THEY HAVE NINE HUNDRED CHARIOTS, AND WE HAVE ONLY A FEW CRUDE WEAPONS.

A FEW DAYS LATER...

BARAK—THIS IS THE PLAN GOD HAS GIVEN ME. TAKE TEN THOUSAND MEN TO MOUNT TABOR. WHEN KING JABIN HEARS OF THIS HE WILL ORDER HIS ARMY, UNDER SISERA, TO COME OUT AND DESTROY US, BUT WITH GOD'S HELP YOU CAN DEFEAT THEM.

I'LL LEAD THE ARMY, BUT ONLY IF YOU'LL GO WITH US. GOD SPEAKS THROUGH YOU, AND IF YOU ARE THERE, I KNOW GOD WILL HELP US.

79

I'LL GO, BUT BECAUSE YOU DID NOT HAVE THE FAITH TO LEAD BY YOURSELF, BARAK, YOU WILL NOT GET THE CREDIT FOR THE VICTORY. GOD WILL DELIVER JABIN'S GENERAL, SISERA, INTO THE HAND OF A WOMAN.

AFTER A QUICK MARCH, THE ISRAELITES REACH MOUNT TABOR. DEBORAH'S PROPHECY COMES TRUE—THE CANAANITE ARMY COMES TO MEET THEM.

HAVE FAITH— FOR THIS IS THE DAY THE LORD WILL DELIVER US!

DEBORAH GIVES THE SIGNAL...AND BARAK CHARGES DOWN THE MOUNTAIN AT THE HEAD OF HIS TROOPS. ABOVE THEM LIGHTNING FLASHES...

A CLOUDBURST TURNS THE PLAIN INTO A SEA OF MUD. THE IRON CHARIOTS OF THE CANAANITE SINK INTO THE MIRE. TRAPPED, THEY ARE AT THE MERCY OF THE ISRAELITES, WHO ATTACK WITH SPEED AND COURAGE.

THE CANAANITES RETREAT.

TO THE RIVER!

WHEN SISERA, GENERAL OF THE CANAANITE FORCES, SEES THAT THEY HAVE BEEN DEFEATED, HE TRIES TO ESCAPE TO A DISTANT CITY. ON THE WAY HE STOPS TO REST IN WHAT HE THINKS IS A FRIENDLY TENT. BUT THE WOMAN WHO LIVES THERE, NAMED JAEL, IS LOYAL TO ISRAEL AND KILLS SISERA WHILE HE IS ASLEEP.

BUT THE KISHON RIVER IS ALREADY OVERFLOWING ITS BANKS... AND THE CANAANITES WHO TRY TO SWIM TO SAFETY SINK UNDER THE WEIGHT OF THEIR HEAVY ARMOR.

WHEN DEBORAH LEARNS THAT THE CANAANITES HAVE BEEN DEFEATED, SHE SINGS A SONG OF VICTORY...

I WILL SING UNTO THE LORD; I WILL SING PRAISES TO THE LORD GOD OF ISRAEL.

THE PEOPLE REJOICE AND SING THEIR PRAISES, TOO. AND FOR FORTY YEARS THERE IS PEACE IN ISRAEL. FAMILIES WORK IN THEIR FIELDS AND HARVEST THEIR CROPS. BUT IN TIME THEY AGAIN FORGET GOD, AND FIND THEMSELVES IN MORE TROUBLE THAN EVER BEFORE.

OUR BIBLE IN PICTURES
Angry Mob of Baal
FROM JUDGES 6: 1-30

IN THE YEARS OF PLENTY THAT FOLLOW DEBORAH'S VICTORY OVER THE CANAANITES, THE ISRAELITES AGAIN FORGET GOD. ONE BY ONE THEY JOIN THEIR NEIGHBORS IN WORSHIPING THE IDOL, BAAL. AT LAST ONLY A FEW MEN IN ALL ISRAEL REMEMBER THAT IT WAS GOD WHO HAD RESCUED THEM FROM THEIR ENEMIES.

ROVING BANDS OF DESERT TRIBESMEN BEGIN TO TERRORIZE THE ISRAELITE VILLAGES, AND RAID THE FIELDS.

RUN FOR YOUR LIVES!

IF THEY FIND WHERE I HID MY GRAIN, WE'LL STARVE.

WHEN THE RAID IS OVER...

IT'S GONE— MY GRAIN, IT'S GONE!

FOR SEVEN LONG YEARS THE ISRAELITES SUFFER AT THE HANDS OF THE DESERT TRIBESMEN. THEY HIDE OUT IN CAVES, THRESH THEIR GRAIN IN SECRET PLACES...BUT ALWAYS THE RAIDERS RETURN.

THEN EVEN MORE FRIGHTENING NEWS COMES...

THE MIDIANITES ARE COMING AGAIN. AND WITH THEM GREAT HORDES FROM THE EAST.

LIKE GRASSHOPPERS THE ENEMY SWARMS OVER THE ISRAELITE FIELDS...STEALING GRAIN, CATTLE, AND SHEEP.

ONE DAY A YOUNG ISRAELITE IS SECRETLY THRESHING HIS GRAIN WHEN A STRANGER APPEARS BEFORE HIM.

WHO ARE YOU? AND WHAT DO YOU WANT?

GOD HAS CHOSEN YOU, GIDEON, TO SAVE YOUR PEOPLE.

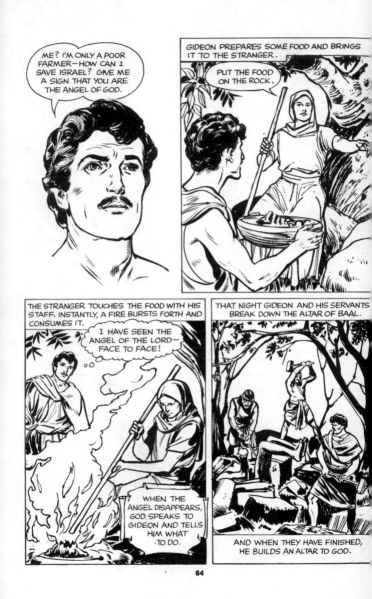

84

Courageous Three Hundred

FROM JUDGES 6: 31—7: 20

AT GOD'S COMMAND, GIDEON TEARS DOWN THE ALTAR OF THE FALSE GOD, BAAL, WHICH HIS FELLOW ISRAELITES WORSHIP. IN ANGER A MOB GOES TO THE HOME OF GIDEON'S FATHER.

COME ON, MEN, LET'S GET HIM!

WE'LL TEACH GIDEON TO DESTROY THE ALTAR OF BAAL.

NO, IF BAAL IS A GOD HE CAN TAKE CARE OF HIMSELF. LET BAAL PUNISH MY SON—IF HE CAN!

THAT SOUNDS FAIR ENOUGH.

ALL ISRAEL WILL SEE THE POWER OF BAAL WHEN HE PUNISHES GIDEON!

THE ISRAELITES WAIT FOR BAAL TO DESTROY GIDEON, BUT AS THE DAYS GO BY, NOTHING HAPPENS. THE ALTAR OF BAAL REMAINS BROKEN. WHEN THE PEOPLE REALIZE THAT BAAL IS ONLY A STONE IDOL, THEY TURN TO GIDEON AS THEIR LEADER.

BUT GIDEON IS STILL NOT SURE THAT HE HAS BEEN CALLED BY GOD. HE ASKS FOR A SIGN.

IF IN THE MORNING THIS WOOL IS WET WITH DEW AND THE GROUND IS DRY, THEN I'LL KNOW THAT I AM THE ONE CHOSEN BY GOD.

THE NEXT MORNING GIDEON HAS HIS SIGN...

THE GROUND IS DRY—BUT THERE'S ENOUGH DEW ON THIS WOOL TO FILL A WHOLE BOWL.

BUT GIDEON IS STILL AFRAID...

O GOD, GIVE ME ONE MORE SIGN. IF IN THE MORNING THE WOOL IS DRY AND THE GROUND IS WET, THEN I'LL KNOW.

THE NEXT MORNING...

THE WOOL IS DRY—AND THE GROUND IS WET! NOW I KNOW THAT I AM THE ONE CALLED TO SAVE MY PEOPLE!

87

GIDEON CALLS THE LEADERS OF ISRAEL TOGETHER.

WITH GOD'S HELP WE CAN DRIVE THE MIDIANITES FROM OUR LAND. ARE YOU WITH ME?

YES!

YES!

WITH AN ARMY OF 32,000 MEN GIDEON MARCHES TO THE HILLS SURROUNDING THE MIDIANITE CAMP.

WHAT A CAMP! THEY HAVE MORE CAMELS THAN THERE ARE SANDS ON THE SHORE.

DON'T WORRY. GOD HAS TOLD ME HOW WE CAN DEFEAT THEM.

GIDEON SPEAKS TO HIS ARMY...

IF ANY OF YOU ARE AFRAID TO FIGHT, LEAVE US NOW AND GO HOME.

ALL BUT 10,000 MEN LEAVE.

GIDEON WATCHES THE MEN WHO ARE LEFT AS THEY DRINK FROM THE BROOK. MOST OF THEM ARE CARELESS AND PUT THEIR FACES DOWN INTO THE WATER. BUT SOME KEEP THEIR HEADS UP, THEIR EYES ALERT—ON THE WATCH FOR DANGER. GIDEON CHOOSES THOSE WHO ARE ALERT—AND SENDS THE REST HOME.

88

ONLY THREE HUNDRED MEN ARE LEFT OUT OF GIDEON'S ARMY OF 32,000 MEN. NOW THE ISRAELITES KNOW BEYOND ALL DOUBT THAT ONLY WITH GOD'S HELP CAN THEY DEFEAT THE ENEMY.

HIDE YOUR TORCHES IN THESE PITCHERS. SPREAD OUT ON THREE SIDES OF THE CAMP. LISTEN FOR MY SIGNAL ON THE TRUMPET.

WE'RE READY.

AT GIDEON'S SIGNAL, THE MEN BLOW THEIR TRUMPETS, SMASH THEIR PITCHERS, WAVE THEIR TORCHES, GIVE THE BATTLE CRY...

THE SWORD OF THE LORD AND OF GIDEON!

AND CHARGE DOWN THE HILL— THREE HUNDRED AGAINST THOUSANDS!

Philistine Raiders

FROM JUDGES 7: 22—13: 1

THE STILLNESS OF THE NIGHT IS SUDDENLY BROKEN BY THE BLARE OF 300 TRUMPETS AND CRASH OF BROKEN PITCHERS. STARTLED FROM THEIR SLEEP, THE MIDIANITES RUSH OUT TO FIND THEIR CAMP ABLAZE WITH FLAMING TORCHES. IN THEIR PANIC THEY EVEN ATTACK ONE ANOTHER...BUT GIDEON AND HIS 300 ISRAELITES SURROUND THE...

WE'VE BEEN ATTACKED!

WHERE'S MY SWORD— MY SHIELD?

THE MIDIANITES THINK THEY HAVE BEEN ATTACKED BY A GIANT ARMY...AND IN TERROR MANY TRY TO ESCAPE TO THE RIVER.

TAKE WORD TO THE TRIBE OF EPHRAIM TO HOLD THE FORDS OF THE JORDAN.

SOME OF THE MIDIANITES REACH THE JORDAN RIVER — BUT THEY ARE CAPTURED BY ISRAELITE SOLDIERS FROM EPHRAIM WAITING IN AMBUSH

IN THE NORTH, GIDEON CHASES THE ENEMY ACROSS THE JORDAN...AND AT LAST ALL OF THE MIDIANITE FORCES ARE DEFEATED.

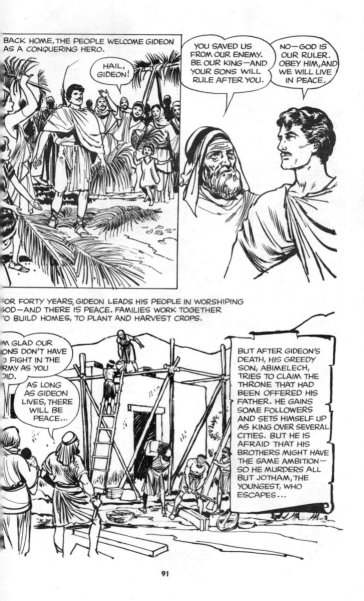

BACK HOME, THE PEOPLE WELCOME GIDEON AS A CONQUERING HERO.

HAIL, GIDEON!

YOU SAVED US FROM OUR ENEMY. BE OUR KING—AND YOUR SONS WILL RULE AFTER YOU.

NO—GOD IS OUR RULER. OBEY HIM, AND WE WILL LIVE IN PEACE.

FOR FORTY YEARS, GIDEON LEADS HIS PEOPLE IN WORSHIPING GOD—AND THERE IS PEACE. FAMILIES WORK TOGETHER TO BUILD HOMES, TO PLANT AND HARVEST CROPS.

I'M GLAD OUR SONS DON'T HAVE TO FIGHT IN THE ARMY AS YOU DID.

AS LONG AS GIDEON LIVES, THERE WILL BE PEACE...

BUT AFTER GIDEON'S DEATH, HIS GREEDY SON, ABIMELECH, TRIES TO CLAIM THE THRONE THAT HAD BEEN OFFERED HIS FATHER. HE GAINS SOME FOLLOWERS AND SETS HIMSELF UP AS KING OVER SEVERAL CITIES. BUT HE IS AFRAID THAT HIS BROTHERS MIGHT HAVE THE SAME AMBITION— SO HE MURDERS ALL BUT JOTHAM, THE YOUNGEST, WHO ESCAPES...

...TO A HIGH HILL OVERLOOKING ONE OF ABIMELECH'S CITIES, AND SHOUTS TO THE PEOPLE.

THE TREES WANTED A KING. THEY ASKED THE OLIVE AND THE FIG, BUT THEY REFUSED BECAUSE THEY WANTED TO KEEP ON BEARING GOOD FRUIT FOR GOD. FINALLY THE TREES ASKED THE BRAMBLE— AND IT ACCEPTED.

THE PEOPLE SOON LEARN THE MEANI OF JOTHAM'S FABLE. THEY FEEL TH PRICK OF THE BRAMBLE KING THEY CHOSE TO RULE OVER THEM.

ABIMELECH TAKES EVEN MY YOUNGEST SON FOR HIS ARMY—HOW CAN WE WORK THE LAND WITHOUT SONS TO HELP US?

BUT THE GREEDY KING DEMANDS MORE AND MORE UNTIL FINALLY THE PEOPLE REVOLT. ABIMELECH SENDS HIS TROOPS TO PUT DOWN THE REVOLT AND TEACH HIS SUBJECTS A LESSON.

WIPE OUT THE CITY—AND DON'T TAKE ANY PRISONERS!

SOME OF THE PEOPLE TAKE REFUGE IN THE TOWER—SO ABIMELECH PREPARES TO SET FIRE TO THE DOOR.

BRING MORE WOOD— WE'LL BURN THEM OUT.

BUT BEFORE THE FIRE CAN BE STARTED, A WOMAN IN THE TOWER DROPS A MILLSTONE ON THE KING'S HEAD. HIS TROOP TURN BACK...AND THE SIEGE IS OVER.

BUT THE EVIL OF ABIMELECH'S RULE CONTINUES. OTHER LEADERS ARISE, BUT THE ISRAELITES CONTINUE TO WORSHIP THE HEATHEN GODS OF THE NATIONS AROUND THEM.

AND AGAIN THEY BECOME SO WEAK THEY CANNOT PROTECT THEMSELVES AGAINST THE ATTACKS OF THEIR NEIGHBORS...

THE PHILISTINES ARE COMING! RUN FOR THE HILLS!

IN TIME MORE AND MORE OF THE ISRAELITES ARE DRIVEN FARTHER INTO THE HILLS.

I GUESS WE'RE SAFE UP HERE.

SURE—BUT ONLY BECAUSE NO ONE WANTS TO LIVE IN THESE ROCKY HILLS.

WHAT CHANCE DO WE HAVE WITH WOODEN SPEARS AGAINST PHILISTINES WITH IRON ONES?

BUT EVEN IN THE HILLS, THE PHILISTINES CONTINUE TO RAID THE VILLAGES.

THIS ONE WILL MAKE A GOOD SLAVE!

MY BOY— GIVE ME BACK MY BOY!

Attacked by a Lion

FROM JUDGES 13: 2—14: 5

THE PHILISTINE RAIDERS STRIKE TIME AND AGAIN AT THE ISRAELITE VILLAGES, CARRYING OFF GRAIN, CATTLE—EVEN CHILDREN TO WORK AS SLAVES. BUT ONE ISRAELITE MOTHER AND FATHER WAIT EAGERLY FOR A STRANGE AND WONDERFUL PROMISE TO COME TRUE. ONE DAY THEY TELL THEIR YOUNG SON, SAMSON, ABOUT IT.

BEFORE YOU WERE BORN, AN ANGEL OF GOD TOLD US THAT SOME DAY YOU WOULD BE THE LEADER OF OUR PEOPLE AND SAVE US FROM THE WICKED PHILISTINES.

I WOULD SAVE OUR PEOPLE? HOW?

WE DON'T KNOW HOW, SON, BUT IF YOU TRUST IN GOD, HE WILL SHOW YOU THE WAY. BUT YOU MUST KEEP A PROMISE YOUR MOTHER MADE TO GOD.

A PROMISE? WHAT IS IT?

TO SET YOU APART AS ONE DEDICATED TO GOD, YOU WILL NEVER CUT YOUR HAIR—OR TOUCH STRONG DRINK.

94

SAMSON KEEPS HIS MOTHER'S PROMISE TO GOD. AND AS THE YEARS PASS AND THE PHILISTINES CONTINUE TO ROB AND PLUNDER THE ISRAELITES, HE DREAMS OF THE DAY WHEN HE CAN SAVE HIS PEOPLE. ONE DAY AFTER A RAID, HE STORMS ANGRILY INTO A MEETING OF THE ELDERS.

THEY KILLED MY COUSIN WITH THIS SPEAR! IT HAS AN IRON HEAD...

YES, THE PHILISTINES KNOW HOW TO MAKE IRON SPEARS, BUT WE DON'T. HOW CAN WE FIGHT THEM WITH WOODEN SPEARS?

SOME DAY I'LL FIGHT THEM, AND WHEN I DO...

HE SNAPPED THAT SPEAR AS IF IT WERE A TWIG.

IF HE IS THAT STRONG NOW, WHAT WILL HE BE LIKE WHEN HE IS A MAN?

AS SAMSON GROWS, HIS STRENGTH GROWS UNTIL AT LAST HE IS THE STRONGEST MAN IN ALL THE TRIBE OF DAN. SOME OF THE PEOPLE WATCH ANXIOUSLY AS HE SETS OUT ONE DAY SEEKING ADVENTURE IN A PHILISTINE VILLAGE.

I HOPE HE DOESN'T GET INTO ANY TROUBLE.

NO MAN IN HIS RIGHT MIND WOULD RISK A FIGHT WITH SAMSON.

NO—NOT ONE MAN, BUT A WHOLE VILLAGE MIGHT. AND THAT COULD MEAN TROUBLE FOR US, TOO.

IN THE VILLAGE OF TIMNATH, SAMSON MEETS A PHILISTINE GIRL.

MAY I GIVE YOU A DRINK OF WATER?

YES, THANK YOU.

SHE'S THE MOST BEAUTIFUL GIRL I'VE EVER SEEN.

IN HER COMPANY SAMSON FORGETS H ANGER TOWARD HER PEOPLE.

WILL YOU MEET ME HERE TOMORROW AT THE SAME TIME?

IF MY FATHER WILL LET ME.

BACK HOME SAMSON LOSES NO TIME TELLING HIS PARENTS WHAT HE WANTS.

I HAVE FALLEN IN LOVE WITH A PHILISTINE GIRL—MAKE ARRANGE-MENTS WITH HER PARENTS FOR OUR MARRIAGE.

MARRIAGE WITH A PHILISTINE?

HOW CAN YOU LOVE ONE OF OUR ENEMIES? SHE DOESN'T BELIEVE IN OUR GOD!

I WANT TO MARRY HEI ANYHOW.

96

SAMSON'S MOTHER AND FATHER TRY TO TALK HIM OUT OF HIS MARRIAGE PLANS, BUT HE WILL NOT LISTEN. AT LAST THEY SET OUT FOR THE VILLAGE OF TIMNATH.

WHY COULDN'T HE HAVE FOUND A GIRL FROM AMONG **OUR** PEOPLE?

HE DIDN'T— AND THERE'S NOTHING WE CAN DO ABOUT IT NOW.

SAMSON IS SO HAPPY AT THE THOUGHT OF SEEING THE GIRL HE LOVES THAT HE FORGETS TO WATCH OUT FOR DANGER...

SUDDENLY HE HEARS AN ANGRY ROAR...HE WHIRLS AROUND AND LOOKS STRAIGHT INTO THE EYES OF A LION...

Samson's Riddle

FROM JUDGES 14: 6-18

ON THE WAY TO ARRANGE FOR HIS MARRIAGE TO A PHILISTINE GIRL, SAMSON IS ATTACKED BY A LION.

WITH HIS BARE HANDS THE STRONG MAN OF ISRAEL KILLS THE LION AND TOSSES IT TO ONE SIDE OF THE PATH.

THANK GOD FOR THE STRENGTH TO DEFEND MYSELF.

IN THE TOWN OF TIMNATH SAMSON'S MOTHER AND FATHER MAKE THE NECESSARY ARRANGEMENTS FOR THE MARRIAGE OF THEIR SON TO THE PHILISTINE GIRL.

HOW SOON WILL YOU COME BACK?

EARLY ON THE DAY OF THE WEDDING.

100

Samson's Revenge

FROM JUDGES 14: 19—15: 12

BACK HOME AS SAMSON'S ANGER COOLS, HE THINKS OF HIS WIFE WAITING FOR HIM.

IT WASN'T HER FAULT. THEY FORCED HER TO TELL THE ANSWER. I'LL GO TO HER AND TELL HER I'M SORRY.

IN THE PHILISTINE CITY HE GOES STRAIGHT TO THE HOME OF HIS WIFE'S FATHER.

I'VE COME TO SEE MY WIFE.

YOUR WIFE? WE THOUGHT YOU HATED HER. SHE IS NOW MARRIED TO YOUR BEST MAN.

HERE IS HER YOUNGER SISTER--SHE'S EVEN MORE BEAUTIFUL. DO YOU WANT TO MARRY HER?

NO! I SHOULD HAVE KNOWN BETTER THAN TO TRUST A PHILISTINE. WHATEVER I DO NOW YOU WILL HAVE COMING TO YOU.

ON THE WAY HOME, HE GOES THROUGH FIELDS RICH WITH RIPENED GRAIN.

FIELDS AND VINEYARDS STOLEN FROM MY PEOPLE! I KNOW HOW I CAN MAKE THE PHILISTINES SORRY FOR WHAT THEY DID TO ME.

102

SAMSON TAKES HIS REVENGE AND ESCAPES THE CITY. THIS TIME THE PHILISTINES SEND OUT AN ARMY TO TRACK HIM DOWN.

HE IS HIDING IN A CAVE IN ETAM ROCK IN JUDAH.

JUDAH? WE'RE MASTER OVER JUDAH. WE'LL MAKE THEM TURN SAMSON OVER TO US.

THE PHILISTINE ARMY SETS UP CAM IN THE SHADOW OF THE ETAM ROCK.

WE HAVE COME FOR SAMSON. HE'S HIDING IN A CAVE IN THAT ROCK. BRING HIM TO US, OR...

SPARE US, AN WE'LL DO AS YOU ASK.

THE MEN OF JUDAH WANT NO TROUBLE WITH THE PHILISTINES, SO THEY SEARCH OUT SAMSON.

GIVE MYSELF UP? TO PHILISTINES WHO WANT TO KILL ME?

WE HAVE NO CHOICE--IT'S EITHER YOU OR ALL THE MEN, WOMEN AND CHILDREN OF JUDAH.

FOR YOUR SAKE, I WILL SURRENDER.

he Gaza Trap

WHEN THE PHILISTINE ARMY DEMANDS THAT THE TRIBE OF JUDAH TURN SAMSON OVER TO THEM, THE TRIBAL LEADERS AGREE. "IT'S YOU," THEY TELL SAMSON, "OR EVERY MAN, WOMAN AND CHILD IN JUDAH." SO SAMSON SURRENDERS...

THAT OUGHT TO DO IT. THE ROPES ARE NEW, AND THE KNOTS ARE TIGHT. HE'S HELPLESS-- LET'S GO.

O GOD, BE WITH ME WHEN I FACE MY ENEMY.

IT'S A GREAT MOMENT FOR THE PHILISTINES WHEN SAMSON IS BOUND AND DELIVERED INTO THEIR HANDS.

WONDER HOW THE STRONG MAN FEELS NOW?

I'D LIKE TO BE THE FIRST ONE TO GET EVEN WITH HIM.

NOT I-- I DON'T TRUST ROPES TO HOLD SAMSON.

WAIT TILL WE SHOW THE MIGHTY MAN OF JUDAH TO THE PEOPLE BACK HOME.

THAT JAWBONE-- IT'S JUST WHAT I NEED!

SUDDENLY, SAMSON BURSTS THE ROPES... AND SEIZES THE JAWBONE OF AN ASS.

NOW WHAT ARE YOU GOING TO SHOW THE PEOPLE BACK HOME?

WITH DEADLY AIM SAMSON STRIKES DOWN ONE PHILISTINE SOLDIER AFTER ANOTHER. THOSE WHO CAN, RUN FOR THEIR LIVES. IN A SHORT WHILE THE ONE-MAN ATTACK IS OVER ...

THEN, WEARY AND THIRSTY, SAMSON PRAYS TO GOD.

LORD, YOU GAVE ME THE VICTORY. DON'T LET ME NOW DIE OF THIRST.

OUR BIBLE IN PICTURES

The Big Bribe

FROM JUDGES 16: 3-5

AT MIDNIGHT SAMSON WALKS DOWN THE STREET AND TOWARD THE GATE...

HMM--HEAVY GUARD ON DUTY TONIGHT. CAN'T BE THAT THEY WANT TO HELP ME THROUGH THE GATE, SO...

WHEN THE PHILISTINES LEARN THAT SAMSON IS IN THEIR CITY THEY CALL OUT ALL THE GUARDS AND LIE IN WAIT FOR HIM.

I'VE NEVER SEEN SAMSON. WHAT'S HE LIKE?

LIKE ANYBODY ELSE--EXCEPT THAT HIS HAIR IS LONG AND HIS STRENGTH IS GREATER THAN A HUNDRED MEN.

I'LL HELP MYSELF!

STOP HIM! DON'T LET HIM GET AWAY!

109

110

111

113

OUR BIBLE IN PICTURES
Samson's Victory
FROM JUDGES 16: 21-30

BETRAYED BY DELILAH, SAMSON IS CAPTURED BY THE PHILISTINES, BLINDED, AND MADE TO GRIND GRAIN IN THE PRISON AT GAZA. BUT—UNNOTICED BY HIS CAPTORS— HIS HAIR BEGINS TO GROW...

O GOD, GIVE ME ONE MORE CHANCE TO FREE MY PEOPLE FROM THE SLAVERY OF THE PHILISTINES!

OUTSIDE THE PRISON WALLS, THE PHILISTINES PREPARE FOR A GREAT FESTIVAL TO DAGON, THEIR GOD.

BRING YOUR GIFTS TO DAGON WHO DELIVERED SAMSON INTO OUR HANDS.

DURING THE FEAST...

WHAT CAN WE DO TO PLEASE THE CROWD?

I HAVE IT—BRING SAMSON OUT AN LET THE PEOPLE HAVE THEIR FUN WITH HIM.

115

O GOD, JUST ONCE MORE, GIVE ME THE STRENGTH I NEED.

AND NOW, LET ME DIE WITH THE PHILISTINES.

USING ALL HIS MIGHTY STRENGTH, SAMSON PUSHES AGAINST THE PILLARS—AND THE GIANT TEMPLE TO THE HEATHEN GOD, DAGON, CRASHES TO THE GROUND. CRUSHED BENEATH IT ARE THE PHILISTINES WHO HAD MADE SLAVES OF SAMSON'S PEOPLE...

BUT THE FIGHT IS NOT YET OVER...AND IN THE MIDST OF THESE TROUBLESOME TIMES THERE COMES A WOMAN FROM A FOREIGN LAND WHO GIVES ISRAEL A VICTORIOUS KING.

"WITH a SICKLE and the WIND"

MAY AND JUNE, THE BEGINNING OF THE LONG, DRY SEASON IN PALESTINE, WERE THE HARVEST MONTHS IN JESUS' TIME. THE HARVESTING WAS DONE BY HAND WITH SICKLES, LIKE THOSE STILL USED TODAY. MANY OF THE POORER PEOPLE HAD TO USE FLINT-BLADED SICKLES, AS IRON WAS EXPENSIVE...SOME PULLED THE WHEAT UP BY ITS ROOTS!

AFTER CUTTING (OR PULLING) THE WHEAT WAS BOUND INTO SHEAVES AND CARRIED TO WHERE IT WAS TO BE THRESHED— AN OPEN PLACE WITH A HARD-PACKED, SMOOTH FLOOR NEAR THE VILLAGE.

ON THE CIRCULAR THRESHING FLOOR THE PATIENT OXEN WERE DRIVEN 'ROUND AND 'ROUND OVER THE WHEAT SHEAVES. THE GRAIN WAS TRODDEN OUT, THE STRAW BROKEN. GRAIN AND CHAFF WERE PILED IN THE CENTER OF THE THRESHING FLOOR—THEN THE GRAIN WINNOWED.

WINNOWING WAS DONE BY TOSSING THE THRESHED GRAIN INTO THE AIR WHERE THE BREEZE BLEW AWAY THE CHAFF. THE HEAVIER GRAIN FELL TO THE FLOOR. WHAT A DIFFERENCE BETWEEN THIS AND TODAY'S HUGE COMBINES WHICH REAP, THRESH AND WINNOW ACRES OF GRAIN IN ONE OPERATION.

AFTER ALL THE GRAIN WAS THRESHED AND WINNOWED IT WAS PUT THROUGH A SIEVE AND THEN STORED. SEED FROM THE TARES, A WEED JESUS OFTEN MENTIONED IN HIS PARABLES, WAS PICKED OUT OF THE GRAIN BY HAND.

OFTEN THE FARMER SLEPT BESIDE HIS STORED GRAIN TO PREVENT ITS BEING STOLEN.

MOST OF THE SMALL FARMS IN PALESTINE WERE WORKED BY THE FARMER'S FAMILY. BUT MANY MEN WHO DID NOT OWN FARMS WOULD HIRE THEMSELVES OUT AS FARM WORKERS. JESUS REFERRED TO THEM IN HIS PARABLE OF THE HOUSEHOLDER WHO HIRED SUCH WORKERS (MATTHEW 20:1).

WHEN ALL THE HARVEST HAD BEEN BROUGHT IN, THE JEWS IN PALESTINE OBSERVED "THE FEAST OF THE TABERNACLES." THIS WAS A SEVEN-DAY PERIOD OF FEASTING TO REMIND THE PEOPLE OF THE TIME WHEN THEY LIVED IN TENTS IN THE WILDERNESS AFTER FLEEING FROM EGYPT. THEY BUILT SMALL SHELTERS OF BRUSH ON THEIR HOUSETOPS AND LIVED IN THEM FOR THE SEVEN DAYS. JESUS MUST HAVE OBSERVED THIS FEAST AS A BOY; JOHN 7:1-17 TELLS OF HIS OBSERVING IT WHEN HE WAS GROWN UP.

Famine

FROM RUTH 1: 1-5

THE BOOK OF RUTH BEGINS WITH A FAMINE IN ISRAEL. IN THE TOWN OF BETHLEHEM...

DON'T CRY—THERE WILL BE SOME FOOD FOR US TODAY.

WE **HAVE** TO HAVE FOOD! WE'VE HAD NOTHING SINCE YESTERDAY. I'LL TRADE YOU MY DONKEY—ANYTHING...

THE FOOD IS GONE—AND I DON'T KNOW WHERE I CAN GET ANY MORE.

WHAT CAN I DO? MY CHILD WILL STARVE!

GO—WHILE YOU HAVE STRENGTH TO TRAVEL—TO SOME FOREIGN LAND WHERE CROPS ARE GOOD.

SO FAMILIES PACK UP THEIR BELONGINGS AND SET OUT, HOPING TO FIND FOOD ALONG THE WAY UNTIL THEY CAN REACH A LAND WHERE THERE IS PLENTY...

IN THE CARAVAN THAT LEAVES BETHLEHEM ARE ELIMELECH, NAOMI, AND THEIR TWO SONS, MAHLON AND CHILION.

WE'LL CROSS THE JORDAN HERE, THEN GO DOWN TO MOAB. TRAVELERS SAY THE CROPS ARE GOOD THERE.

MOAB? THE PEOPLE THERE DON'T BELIEVE IN OUR GOD!

IN THE FOREIGN LAND OF MOAB, ELIMELECH AND THE BOYS FIND WORK IN THE GRAIN FIELDS...

O GOD, WE THANK THEE FOR THIS FOOD.

HARVEST SEASONS COME AND GO—FOOD IS PLENTIFUL, AND THE ISRAELITE FAMILY PROSPERS. THEN—SUDDENLY—ELIMELECH DIES.

NAOMI IS HEARTBROKEN...

AS LONG AS WE LIVE, MOTHER, YOU WILL NEVER WANT FOR FOOD OR CARE.

HOW FORTUNATE I AM TO HAVE SONS LIKE YOU.

BUT NAOMI WATCHES WITH ANXIOUS EYES AS HER SONS MAKE FRIENDS WITH TWO GIRLS IN THE VILLAGE.

RUTH IS A GOOD GIRL—BUT SHE IS A FOREIGNER. MY SONS SHOULD MARRY GIRLS FROM AMONG OUR OWN PEOPLE.

BUT IN SPITE OF ALL NAOMI CAN DO, THE BOYS FALL IN LOVE WITH THE MOABITE GIRLS...AND ONE DAY...

MOTHER, RUTH HAS JUST PROMISED TO BE MY WIFE!

GOD BLESS YOU BOTH AND GIVE YOU HAPPINESS.

OH, WHY COULDN'T MY SONS HAVE MARRIED GIRLS WHO WOULD SHARE OUR RELIGION!

NAOMI'S SONS MARRY AND THE MOABITE GIRLS COME TO LIVE IN HER HOME. THEN—WITHOUT WARNING—AN EPIDEMIC STRIKES THE VILLAGE. MAHLON AND CHILION TAKE SICK.

THE FEVER IS WORSE!

MY SONS, MY SONS. I CANNO LIVE WITHOUT THEM!

BY MORNING, MAHLON AND CHILION ARE DEAD.

Stranger in Bethlehem

FROM RUTH 1: 6—2: 5

THE EPIDEMIC THAT SWEPT THROUGH MOAB IS OVER, BUT IN MANY VILLAGES FAMILIES STILL MOURN THE LOSS OF THEIR LOVED ONES...

ISN'T THAT THE HOME OF NAOMI, THE ISRAELITE WOMAN WHO LOST HER TWO SONS?

YES, I WONDER WHAT SHE WILL DO NOW? LIFE ISN'T EASY FOR A WIDOW WITHOUT SONS, ESPECIALLY IN A FOREIGN LAND.

INSIDE THE HOUSE, NAOMI MAKES HER PLANS.

TRAVELERS SAY CROPS ARE GOOD AGAIN IN BETHLEHEM. I'LL GO BACK HOME—MY DAUGHTERS-IN-LAW DON'T NEED ME HERE.

THE NEXT MORNING...

YOU HAVE BEEN KIND TO ME—AND I LOVE YOU BOTH, BUT MOAB HAS NEVER BEEN MY REAL HOME. I'M GOING BACK TO BETHLEHEM.

WE UNDERSTAND, MOTHER, AND WE'LL GO WITH YOU.

123

THEY SET OUT, AND ON THE BORDER OF MOAB...

IT IS TIME TO SAY GOOD-BY. YOU ARE BOTH YOUNG, AND I HOPE THAT YOU WILL MARRY AGAIN AND HAVE HOMES OF YOUR OWN. MAY GOD BE KIND TO YOU, AS YOU HAVE BEEN TO ME.

ORPAH BIDS NAOMI GOOD-BY, BUT RUTH...

DON'T ASK ME TO LEAVE YOU. WHEREVER YOU GO, I'LL GO WITH YOU. YOUR PEOPLE WILL BE MY PEOPLE AND YOUR GOD MY GOD! NOTHING BUT DEATH WILL PART US.

RUTH'S WORDS BRING TEARS TO NAOMI'S EYES... WITH A PRAYER OF THANKFULNESS SHE ACCEPTS RUTH'S DECISION. TOGETHER THEY WALK ON UNTIL THEY REACH NAOMI'S OLD HOME —THE CITY OF BETHLEHEM.

HOME AT LAST! WILL MY FRIENDS KNOW ME—AND WELCOME ME HOME?

THIS IS THE CITY THAT WILL BE MY HOME—NOW I KNOW HOW NAOMI FELT ABOUT BEING A STRANGER IN MOAB!

INSIDE THE GATES OF BETHLEHEM PEOPLE STARE IN AMAZEMENT.

ARE YOU NAOMI? HOW YOU HAVE CHANGED!

YES, I LEFT BETHLEHEM WITH A HUSBAND AND TWO SONS— I RETURN WITH ONLY A DAUGHTER-IN-LAW TO HELP ME.

124

125

Naomi's Strategy

FROM RUTH 2: 6—3: 18

THE GLEANERS WATCH EAGERLY AS BOAZ, THE OWNER OF THE FIELDS, QUESTIONS HIS FOREMAN ABOUT THE YOUNG WOMAN GATHERING GRAIN IN HIS FIELDS.

HER NAME IS RUTH—SHE IS THE MOABITE WOMAN WHO TAKES CARE OF HER MOTHER-IN-LAW, NAOMI.

HOW BEAUTIFUL SHE IS!

I HAVE HEARD HOW KIND YOU ARE TO YOUR MOTHER-IN-LAW. GLEAN IN MY FIELDS AS MUCH AS YOU LIKE—AND MAY GOD REWARD AND PROTECT YOU.

THANK YOU. YOU ARE VERY KIND.

AT LUNCH TIME BOAZ INVITES RUTH TO EAT WITH HIM AND HIS REAPERS...

127

128

Ancestress of a King

NEXT MORNING BOAZ WATCHES FOR THE RELATIVE WHO HAS FIRST RIGHT TO BUY THE LAND THAT BELONGED TO NAOMI'S DEAD HUSBAND—AND TO MARRY RUTH.

GOOD MORNING! WILL YOU STOP AND DISCUSS A MATTER THAT IS IMPORTANT TO BOTH OF US?

GOOD MORNING TO YOU, BOAZ. WHAT IS THE PROBLEM?

WHEN THE MAN IS SEATED BOAZ INVITES THE ELDERS OF THE CITY TO JOIN THEM...

THE LAND THAT BELONGED TO NAOMI'S HUSBAND IS FOR SALE. ONE OF US MUST BUY IT TO KEEP IT IN THE FAMILY. YOU ARE THE CLOSEST RELATIVE... WILL YOU BUY THE LAND?

YES, I WILL BUY IT!

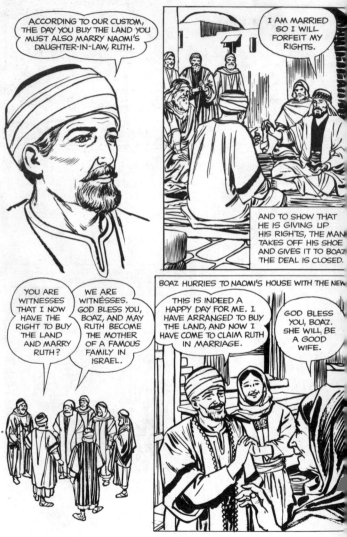

ACCORDING TO OUR CUSTOM, THE DAY YOU BUY THE LAND YOU MUST ALSO MARRY NAOMI'S DAUGHTER-IN-LAW, RUTH.

I AM MARRIED SO I WILL FORFEIT MY RIGHTS.

AND TO SHOW THAT HE IS GIVING UP HIS RIGHTS, THE MAN TAKES OFF HIS SHOE AND GIVES IT TO BOAZ. THE DEAL IS CLOSED.

YOU ARE WITNESSES THAT I NOW HAVE THE RIGHT TO BUY THE LAND AND MARRY RUTH?

WE ARE WITNESSES. GOD BLESS YOU, BOAZ, AND MAY RUTH BECOME THE MOTHER OF A FAMOUS FAMILY IN ISRAEL.

BOAZ HURRIES TO NAOMI'S HOUSE WITH THE NEWS

THIS IS INDEED A HAPPY DAY FOR ME. I HAVE ARRANGED TO BUY THE LAND, AND NOW I HAVE COME TO CLAIM RUTH IN MARRIAGE.

GOD BLESS YOU, BOAZ. SHE WILL BE A GOOD WIFE.

OUR BIBLE IN PICTURES

Call in the Night

FROM I SAMUEL 1: 1—3: 17

AT THE TABERNACLE AT SHILOH, ELI, THE HIGH PRIEST, WATCHES THE FAITHFUL COME TO WORSHIP. HE NOTICES A WOMAN AND SUDDENLY HE BECOMES ANGRY...

SHE ACTS AS IF SHE'S DRUNK! HOW DARE SHE INSULT GOD!

HUNDREDS OF YEARS HAVE PASSED SINCE THE ISRAELITES SETTLED IN THE PROMISED LAND OF CANAAN. DURING THAT TIME THEY OFTEN TURNED FROM GOD TO WORSHIP HEATHEN IDOLS. AS A RESULT THEY HAVE BECOME WEAK—ALMOST SLAVES OF THEIR ENEMIES, THE PHILISTINES. TO SOME IT SEEMS THAT GOD HAS FORGOTTEN HIS PROMISE TO MAKE ISRAEL STRONG.

THE BOOK OF I SAMUEL BEGINS..

ANGRILY HE ACCUSES HER...

NO! NO! I AM NOT DRUNK, I AM UNHAPPY; AND IN MY SORROW I HAVE POURED OUT MY HEART TO GOD, ASKING HIM TO HELP ME.

GO IN PEACE, HANNAH, AND MAY GOD GRANT THEE THY PRAYER.

HANNAH IS SO HAPPY THAT SHE RUSHES OUT OF THE TABERNACLE TO FIND HER HUSBAND.

OH, ELKANAH, I PRAYED TO GOD FOR A SON— AND ELI BLESSED ME AND ASKED GOD TO GIVE ME WHAT I PRAYED FOR.

A SON? I, TOO, PRAY THAT GOD WILL GRANT YOUR PRAYER.

GOD ANSWERS HANNAH'S PRAYER AND WHEN THE BOY IS OLD ENOUGH TO LEAVE HIS MOTHER, SHE BRINGS HIM TO ELI.

WHEN I ASKED GOD FOR A SON, I PROMISED THAT HE WOULD SERVE THE LORD ALL HIS LIFE. SO I HAVE BROUGHT HIM HERE TO BE TRAINED IN GOD'S HOUSE. HIS NAME IS SAMUEL.

GOD BLESS YOU, HANNAH. LEAVE THE BOY WITH ME AND I WILL TEACH HIM TO BE A SERVANT OF THE LORD.

SAMUEL STAYS WITH ELI AND EAGERLY LEARNS WHAT GOD EXPECTS OF THOSE WHO SERVE HIM. EACH YEAR WHEN HANNAH AND HER HUSBAND COME TO WORSHIP, SHE BRINGS SAMUEL A NEW COAT.

IT'S JUST LIKE A PRIEST'S ROBE. THANK YOU, MOTHER.

OLD ELI IS PROUD OF SAMUEL—BUT HE IS BROKENHEARTED WHEN HE THINKS OF HIS OWN TWO SONS. AS PRIESTS, THEY HAVE SINNED AGAINST GOD AND CHEATED THE PEOPLE. ELI KNOWS THAT HE, TOO, IS GUILTY BECAUSE HE HAS DONE NOTHING TO STOP THEM.

134

a Heathen Temple

ELI, THE HIGH PRIEST OF ISRAEL, KNOWS THAT GOD HAS SPOKEN TO HIS YOUNG HELPER, SAMUEL. SAMUEL DOESN'T WANT TO REPEAT THE MESSAGE, BUT ELI INSISTS...

GOD SAID, "ELI'S SONS ARE WICKED AND ELI HAS NOT TRIED TO STOP THEM. THEY WILL BE PUNISHED FOR THE EVIL THEY HAVE DONE."

THE LORD WILL DO WHAT IS JUST.

WORD SPREADS THAT GOD HAS SPOKEN TO SAMUEL. AND AS SAMUEL GROWS UP ALL ISRAEL KNOWS THAT HE IS A TRUE PROPHET OF GOD.

SUDDENLY WAR BREAKS OUT WITH THE PHILISTINES. A FIERCE BATTLE RAGES, AND THE ISRAELITES ARE BADLY DEFEATED.

IF ONLY OUR PRIESTS WERE MEN OF GOD LIKE SAMUEL. HOW LONG MUST WE SUFFER UNDER THE LYING AND CHEATING OF ELI'S SONS?

MARK MY WORDS, THEY WILL BRING ABOUT THEIR OWN DESTRUCTION.

WE'VE LOST FOUR THOUSAND MEN.

WHAT CAN WE DO?

135

136

137

The Turning Point

FROM I SAMUEL 5: 3—7: 10

WITH SHOUTS OF TRIUMPH THE PHILISTINES PLACE THE SACRED ARK OF GOD IN THEIR HEATHEN TEMPLE. TO THEM IT IS A SIGN THAT THE PHILISTINE GOD, DAGON, HAS CONQUERED THE GOD OF ISRAEL. BUT THE NEXT MORNING THE IDOL LIES ON ITS FACE BEFORE THE ARK. PRIESTS REPLACE THE IDOL, AND ON THE FOLLOWING MORNING...

LOOK! OUR GREAT GOD, DAGON, LIES BROKEN BEFORE THE ARK OF THE ISRAELITES!

SO THE ARK IS TAKEN FROM ONE PHILISTINE CITY TO ANOTHER...AND IN EACH CITY A PLAGUE BREAKS OUT...

NOT A FAMILY HAS ESCAPED THIS STRANGE ILLNESS.

OUR FIELDS ARE OVER RUN WITH MICE. I TELL YOU—A CURSE HAS BEEN PUT UPON THIS CITY.

THE PHILISTINES SOON REALIZE THAT THEIR TROUBLES BEGAN WHEN THEY CAPTURED THE HOLY ARK OF ISRAEL. FINALLY THEY RETURN THE ARK TO ISRAEL, BUT ISRAEL IS WORSHIPING IDOLS. THE ARK IS PLACED IN A HOUSE AND ALMOST FORGOTTEN.

BUT AFTER YEARS OF STRUGGLE UNDER THE PHILISTINES, THE ISRAELITES ARE READY TO LISTEN WHEN SAMUEL SPEAKS...

RETURN TO THE LORD! WORSHIP HIM WITH ALL YOUR HEARTS, AND GOD WILL DELIVER YOU FROM THE PHILISTINES.

SAMUEL IS RIGHT! LET US THROW AWAY OUR IDOLS·AND WORSHIP GOD.

LET US ALL GO TO THE CITY OF MIZPEH AND PRAY TOGETHER!

EAGERLY THE PEOPLE FOLLOW THIS MAN WHO SPEAKS BOLDLY FOR GOD. BY THE THOUSANDS THEY SET OUT...

BUT THE GREAT MARCH TO MIZPEH IS DISCOVERED BY THE PHILISTINES.

IF THOUSANDS OF ISRAELITES ARE MASSING AT MIZPEH IT CAN MEAN ONLY ONE THING — THEY PLAN TO ATTACK US.

LET'S STRIKE BEFORE THEY DO, AND **THIS** TIME WE'LL CRUSH THEM SO BADLY THEY'LL NEVER FIGHT AGAIN!

139

MEANTIME, AT MIZPEH, THE ISRAELITES ASSEMBLE BEFORE AN ALTAR TO GOD.

FORGIVE THY PEOPLE, LORD, AND HELP THEM. THEY HAVE TORN DOWN THE IDOLS, AND REPENTED FOR HAVING TURNED AWAY FROM THEE.

SUDDENLY A LOUD SHOUT RINGS THROUGH THE CAMP...

HELP! THE PHILISTINES ARE COMING!

ASK GOD TO SAVE US, SAMUEL— OR WE WILL ALL BE KILLED!

OUR BIBLE IN PICTURES
A Prophet Speaks
FROM I SAMUEL 7: 10—9: 20

THE PHILISTINE ARMY PREPARES FOR A RUSH ATTACK ON THE ISRAELITES GATHERED AT MIZPEH. ON THE HILLTOP SAMUEL OFFERS A SACRIFICE AND PRAYS TO GOD FOR HELP.

THIS TIME WE'LL TEACH THEM A LESSON THEY WON'T FORGET.

BUT WHEN THE PHILISTINES ARE WITHIN BATTLE RANGE, A SUDDEN STORM BREAKS...

WE CAN FIGHT THE ISRAELITES, BUT WE CAN'T FIGHT THE GOD OF THUNDER AND LIGHTNING!

GOD HAS ANSWERED OUR PRAYER.

LET'S GO AFTER THEM.

THE PHILISTINE· DEFEAT IS A TURNING POINT IN ISRAEL'S HISTORY—NEVER AGAIN DO THE PHILISTINES INVADE ISRAEL WHILE SAMUEL IS ITS LEADER. TO REMIND HIS PEOPLE THAT IT WAS GOD WHO HELPED THEM WIN THEIR VICTORY, SAMUEL ERECTS A STONE WHICH HE CALLS EBENEZER (STONE OF HELP).

FOR YEARS SAMUEL JUDGES THE PEOPLE OF ISRAEL, AND THERE IS PEACE. BUT AS HE GROWS OLD THE TRIBAL LEADERS BECOME WORRIED...

SAMUEL, YOU ARE GROWING OLD, AND YOUR SONS ARE NOT WORTHY TO TAKE YOUR PLACE AS JUDGE OF ISRAEL. GIVE US A KING LIKE OTHER NATIONS HAVE.

I WILL PRAY TO GOD ABOUT YOUR REQUEST.

LATER—

THE LORD HAS TOLD ME TO WARN YOU WHAT A KING WILL DO—HE WILL SEND YOUR SONS TO BATTLE, YOUR DAUGHTERS WILL BECOME HIS SERVANTS, AND YOUR BEST CROPS WILL BE USED TO FEED HIS COURT.

MAYBE SO, BUT WE STILL WANT A KING!

AGAIN SAMUEL PRAYS TO GOD, THEN—

GOD WANTS ME TO DO AS YOU HAVE ASKED. GO HOME, AND I WILL SEND WORD WHEN I HAVE FOUND A KING FOR YOU.

A FEW DAYS LATER SAMUEL SETS OUT EAGERLY FOR THE GATE OF THE CITY—

YESTERDAY GOD TOLD ME THAT TODAY I WOULD MEET A MAN, HERE, WHO IS THE ONE TO BE THE KING OF ISRAEL.

AT THE GATE, A YOUNG FARMER WHO IS LOOKING FOR HIS LOST DONKEYS STOPS SAMUEL.

I NEED HELP. CAN YOU TELL ME WHERE I MIGHT FIND THE PROPHET, SAMUEL?

I AM THE PROPHET. DON'T WORRY ABOUT YOUR DONKEYS —THEY HAVE BEEN FOUND. COME WITH ME TO WORSHIP THE LORD, AND TOMORROW I WILL TELL YOU WHAT GREAT THINGS ARE IN STORE FOR YOU.

GREAT THINGS— FOR ME? WHAT DOES HE MEAN?

143

Test for a King

FROM I SAMUEL 9: 20—11: 7

THE YOUNG FARMER, SAUL, IS STUNNED WHEN SAMUEL TELLS HIM THAT GREAT THINGS ARE IN STORE FOR HIM. THEY WORSHIP GOD TOGETHER, THEN SAMUEL INVITES SAUL TO A SPECIAL FEAST.

WHY SHOULD THIS YOUNG MAN BE SO HIGHLY HONORED?

SAMUEL MAKES NO EXPLANATION TO HIS GUESTS, BUT EARLY THE NEXT MORNING HE ACCOMPANIES SAUL AND HIS SERVANT AS THEY LEAVE THE CITY.

SEND YOUR SERVANT ON AHEAD, SAUL. I HAVE A MESSAGE FOR YOU FROM GOD.

THE LORD HAS ANOINTED YOU TO RULE OVER HIS PEOPLE. CALL ON THE LORD, AND HE WILL BE WITH YOU.

SURPRISED—AND A LITTLE FRIGHTENED—AT ALL THAT HAS HAPPENED TO HIM, SAUL STARTS HOME. BUT ON THE WAY THE SPIRIT OF GOD COMES TO HIM. HOWEVER, WHEN HE REACHES HOME, HE DOES NOT TELL ANYONE THAT HE HAS BEEN ANOINTED KING!

WHEN SAMUEL CALLS THE PEOPLE TO MIZPEH, SAUL GOES, TOO. BEFORE ALL ISRAEL SAMUEL MAKES A SURPRISING ANNOUNCEMENT.

GOD HAS CHOSEN SAUL TO RULE OVER YOU.

WHERE IS HE?

SEARCH IS QUICKLY MADE, AND SAUL—WHO IS AWED BY THE THOUGHT OF BEING KING—IS FOUND HIDING.

WHEN HE IS BROUGHT FORTH, THE PEOPLE SHOUT: LONG LIVE THE KING!

AT MIZPEH THE PEOPLE SHOUTED THEIR PRAISES TO SAUL—BUT AFTER HE RETURNS HOME, SOME COMPLAIN.

FINE THING —THERE GOES OUR KING— BACK TO THE FARM.

HE'LL BE NO HELP TO US.

145

146

WHEN WORD COMES THAT THE AMMONITES HAVE SURROUNDED AN ISRAELITE CITY, SAUL FACES HIS FIRST TEST AS KING. TO HIS AMAZEMENT—AND ANGER—HE DISCOVERS THAT SOME OF HIS PEOPLE ARE AFRAID TO FIGHT! HE ACTS AT ONCE...

BY ORDER OF THE KING WE ARE TO KILL THE OXEN OF ANY MAN WHO REFUSES TO DEFEND HIS COUNTRY!

ER—I'LL JOIN THE ARMY RIGHT NOW!

N ARMY IS QUICKLY FORMED, ND SAUL ATTACKS AT DAWN. AUGHT BY SURPRISE, THE MMONITES ARE DEFEATED.

147

148

BUT WHEN WORD REACHES THE MAIN ARMY OF THE PHILISTINES...

TAKE THIRTY THOUSAND CHARIOTS, SIX THOUSAND HORSEMEN AND ALL OUR INFANTRY—SET UP A CAMP AT MICHMASH. FROM THERE WE CAN SEND OUT RAIDING PARTIES THAT WILL DRAW SAUL FROM HIS STRONGHOLD AT GILGAL.

IN SPITE OF FORMER VICTORIES MANY OF THE ISRAELITES LOSE COURAGE WHEN THEY SEE THE SIZE OF THE ENEMY FORCES.

THE PHILISTINES OUTNUMBER US BY THOUSANDS. I'M HIDING OUT UNTIL THIS IS OVER.

THERE'S A PIT DOWN THE VALLEY— I'LL HIDE THERE.

EVEN IN THE CAMP OF KING SAUL, THE SOLDIERS ARE AFRAID.

A RAID ON A PHILISTINE GARRISON IS ONE THING—FIGHTING THE WHOLE PHILISTINE ARMY IS ANOTHER.

THE MEN ARE LOSING THEIR NERVE. WE CAN'T WAIT MUCH LONGER FOR SAMUEL TO COME AND OFFER THE SACRIFICE TO GOD.

YOU'RE RIGHT. WE'LL WAIT NO LONGER. I'LL MAKE THE OFFERING!

149

The King Disobeys

THE ISRAELITES WATCH WITH GROWING TERROR AS THE PHILISTINE ARMY SETS UP CAMP AT MICHMASH. SAUL, AFRAID THAT HIS PEOPLE WILL PANIC, LOSES FAITH IN GOD'S GUIDANCE. INSTEAD OF WAITING FOR SAMUEL TO OFFER THE SACRIFICE, HE MAKES THE OFFERING HIMSELF. HE NO SOONER FINISHES THAN HE SEES SAMUEL COMING...

I WAS AFRAID MY PEOPLE WOULD FLEE BEFORE YOU GOT HERE, SO I OFFERED THE SACRIFICE.

YOU HAVE DISOBEYED GOD. YOU CAN DO THAT AN[D] HOLD YOU[R] KINGDOM

MEANTIME—INSTEAD OF MAKING AN OPEN ATTACK, THE PHILISTINES SEND OUT RAIDING PARTIES TO DRAW SAUL FROM CAMP—BUT SAUL WILL NOT COME OUT. HIS SON, PRINCE JONATHAN, DECIDES TO TAKE ACTION...

LET'S ATTACK THE PHILISTINE GARRISON BY OURSELVES.

I'M WITH YOU!

ECRETLY JONATHAN AND HIS ARMOR-BEARER EAVE CAMP. WHEN THEY REACH THE FOOT OF HE CLIFF THAT LEADS TO THE PHILISTINE ARRISON, THE ENEMY DARES THEM TO COME P AND FIGHT. BOLDLY, JONATHAN AND HIS RIEND SCALE THE CLIFF...

FOLLOW ME, FOR WITH THE LORD THERE IS NO NEED FOR LARGE NUMBERS.

AT THE TOP THEY ATTACK WITH SUCH DARING THAT THE PHILISTINES FLEE IN PANIC. IN THEIR CONFUSION, THE PHILISTINES EVEN ATTACK ONE ANOTHER.

WHEN SAUL LEARNS THE PHILISTINES ARE RETREATING, AND DISCOVERS THAT IT IS JONATHAN WHO HAS ATTACKED THEM, HE LEADS HIS ARMY AGAINST THE ENEMY AND DRIVES THEM BACK TO THEIR OWN COUNTRY.

AFTER THIS VICTORY, SAUL ATTACKS THE OTHER ENEMIES OF ISRAEL AND DRIVES THEM AWAY. BUT THE RAIDS OF THE DESERT TRIBE OF THE AMALEKITES CONTINUE —

151

152

OUR BIBLE IN PICTURES
A Mysterious Visit
FROM I SAMUEL 15: 15—16: 11

SAUL HAS BEEN COMMANDED BY SAMUEL TO BRING HOME NO SPOILS FROM HIS VICTORY. BUT HE CANNOT RESIST THE FAT SHEEP AND CATTLE. HE BRINGS THEM HOME—AND IS CAUGHT RED-HANDED BY SAMUEL.

MY PEOPLE TOOK ONLY THE BEST TO SACRIFICE TO GOD.

TO OBEY IS BETTER THAN TO SACRIFICE. THIS IS THE SECOND TIME YOU HAVE DISOBEYED GOD. AND BECAUSE YOU HAVE DONE SO, THE LORD WILL TAKE YOUR KINGDOM FROM YOU.

NO—MY PEOPLE —I...

AT FIRST SAUL TRIES TO LAY THE BLAME ON HIS PEOPLE, BUT FINALLY HE ADMITS HE HAS SINNED AGAINST GOD. SAMUEL PRAYS WITH SAUL—THEN GOES HOME, NEVER AGAIN TO VISIT THE KING.

YOU'RE A BRAVE SHEPHERD, DAVID. BUT HURRY HOME—SAMUEL WANTS TO SEE YOU. I'VE BROUGHT A MAN TO STAY WITH THE SHEEP.

ME? BUT WHY?

ON THE HIKE BACK TO THE CITY, DAVID CONTINUES TO WONDER. BUT WHEN SAMUEL SEES THE YOUNG SHEPHERD BOY, HE KNOWS HIS SEARCH HAS ENDED, FOR HE HEARS GOD SAY: *"THIS IS MY CHOSEN ONE."*

BEFORE JESSE AND HIS SONS, SAMUEL BLESSES DAVID AND ANOINTS HIS HEAD WITH OIL.

THE LORD BLESS YOU, FOR YOU WILL BE THE NEXT KING OF ISRAEL.

DAVID DOES NOT KNOW WHEN HE WILL BE MADE KING. BUT AS HE GOES BACK TO HIS SHEEP HE HAS A SPECIAL FEELING OF GOD'S PRESENCE WITH HIM.

THE LORD IS MY STRENGTH. WHAT HAVE I TO FEAR?